of

Grace' ⌐ ⌐ary

The Journal of Grace Jane Dexter 1884-93

Edited by Rowena Edlin-White

Grace Jane Dexter Dupree
1865-1963

Published by *smallprint* 2005
an imprint of *Woolgatherings*,
11 Frederick Ave, Carlton, Nottingham NG4 1HP
England, UK

ISBN 1-900074-16-8

Printed by Fineprint, Nottingham NG3 2NJ

Cover photo: Grace Jane Dexter, 1889

In affectionate memory of
Philip Weigel Rest
1915-2003

And with grateful thanks to
Brady Allan, Helen Collins, Jane McCoy & Kenneth Rutt.
Also to Stephen Best, Gilbert Clarke, Jim Freebury,
The Magic Attic, Swadlincote,
Nottinghamshire Archives,
Derbyshire Record Office &
Derbyshire Libraries & Heritage Dept., Matlock.

Acknowledgements

Extract from the Log Book of St Peter's Trust 1874-97 (Ref: SL125/S12/2)
used with permission of Nottinghamshire Archives.
Extracts from Lea School Log Book 1862-88 (Ref: D4335/5/1)
reproduced from original document in Derbyshire Record Office.
Photograph of Sneinton Board School by Jim Freebury, used with permission.
Photographs of John Dexter, Beaty Dexter and Grace's teaching certificate
property of Jane McCoy and used with permission.
All other illustrations property of Rowena Edlin-White

❧Introduction❧

I am fortunate to come from a family which has, in every generation, produced people who write things down: diaries, letters, postcards, even cartoons; and — even better — seldom threw anything away!

In 1957, Grace Jane Dexter Dupree gave this diary to Joyce, sister of my father's cousin, Philip Rest, and the accompanying letter is reproduced on page 4. Twenty years after Joyce's death, Philip obtained the diary from his brother-in-law, Ken Rutt, and gave it to me, because he knew that as a writer myself I would appreciate it. He was right, I do appreciate it, and I find it very exciting; not only because of Grace's friendship with Florence Nightingale, but also for the wealth of domestic and social detail it contains about the life of a young woman training under the old pupil teacher system in the 1880s and 90s. The books she read, the concerts she attended, the preachers she heard and her participation in events of national significance like Queen Victoria's Jubilee, all combine to make Grace's diary an important historical document worthy of a wider readership. To this end, I have prepared it for publication and found much enjoyment in researching the background to the events it describes in and around Nottingham, Derbyshire, Leicestershire and East London.

❧The Dexter Family❧

Around 1840 William Bull Dexter (1788-1850), lace maker, and his wife Jane Smedley (1792-1847), moved from Melbourne, Derbyshire to Nottingham. They had five children: Jane (1815-1917), William (1817-60), Walter (1821-84), John (1827-1904) and Thomas (1828-1901).

The eldest, Jane, was already married to Henry Dawkins. "Aunt Jane" became the matriarch of the family and something of a legend in her own right. Her name appears on many marriage and death certificates of family members — she was always there in times of need. She wrote loving little notes on the occasion of weddings and special birthdays, several of which survive because kept and cherished. She was present at Grace's birth and probably delivered her. She lived to the age of 102, celebrating her centenary in 1915 to great media acclaim, and remained a significant presence to the end of her life, much loved by all the family.

William Dexter Jnr. was an artist. Originally a painter with the Derby China Factory, he married Caroline Harper, author and Bloomerite, and together they pursued a Bohemian lifestyle in Australia, where he died of consumption in 1860. Their story has been ably told by Patrick Morgan in his book *Folie à Deux* (Quakers Hill Press).

Walter Dexter (Grace's "Uncle Walter") was a lace maker and engineer like his father who, in 1871, trade being bad, took his lace machines, wife and eight of his children to Brooklyn, New York. They returned after about four years, but several of the children emigrated permanently or continued to move back and forth between Britain and America for the rest of their lives. Walter Dexter was my great-great grandfather.

Of Thomas Dexter I know little, except that he was also involved in the lace trade.

John Dexter was Grace's father. He married Rebecca Dawkins at Barker Gate Chapel in Nottingham on 29th May 1850. On the 1851 census we find him, aged 24, living in Penn Lane, Melbourne, a Schoolmaster at the National School, with Rebecca (27), a Schoolmistress, and her mother Elizabeth Dawkins. (Rebecca, who was born in Market Rasen, Lincolnshire, was sister to the Henry Dawkins who had married John's sister Jane.) Their first child, Mary Elizabeth, was born the following year in 1852, and Priscilla Jane in 1853. Around 1854 they moved back to Nottingham where John Samuel Esperance was born in 1855. By now John was no longer a teacher but working as an Assurance Clerk. Hepzibah Milton was born in 1857 and Hermon in 1859 and on both their birth certificates John is a Book Keeper.

By 1861 the family was living in Sherwood and John working as a Gasfitter, Painter & Gilder, Plumber & Glazier! It seems to have taken him some time to discover his true profession. Another daughter, Constance Ellen, was born in 1862; but a year later a string of tragic deaths afflicted the Dexters. Constance Ellen died of convulsions in 1863 at the age of 11 months — a death sudden enough for an inquest to be called, but death by natural causes was the verdict. In March 1864 Hermon died of *Tabesmesenterica* (wasting) and asthma, aged four and a half, to be quickly followed in May by Priscilla Jane, aged 10, of consumption.

Into this grieving family Grace Jane was born on 15th September 1865, at 84 Caroline Street in the St. Ann's area of Nottingham. Hepzibah Milton died less than nine months later, aged 8, another victim of consumption.

Fortunately the Grim Reaper claimed no more victims for the time being, and in the 1871 Census John and Rebecca are found living at 19 Clyde Villas, Wilford Road, with Mary (18), John Samuel (17), Clerk, and Grace, aged 5 (Scholar). John Snr. is described as an "Agent". Mary does not have a trade or profession but may have been keeping house for them all, because according to Wright's Trade Directory, by 1874 Rebecca was running a school at 21 Clyde Street, whilst John Snr. had settled into the timber trade at the Steam Saw Mills in Canal Street.

On 29th November 1877, John Samuel married Maria Lane of Market Street, Nottingham, at Osmaston Road Baptist Chapel, Derby, and their first child Constance Maria Beatrice ("Beaty") was born on 26th October 1878. Another daughter, Ethel Grace, was born around June 1880 but died 24th December 1880. Hilda Mary was born around December 1882, but she also died on 19th April 1883, a year after her mother, Maria, whose death is described so poignantly at the beginning of the Diary.

By 1881, John (54) is now Manager in a Saw-mill and living at 1 Burton Street (now Burnham St.) Sherwood, with Rebecca (57), Mary (28) who is a Maker-up of Hosiery, and Grace (15), a Monitor in a Board School.

Grace takes up the story in her diary on 2nd February 1884. The diary covers the next ten years or so: some years she writes regularly and in great detail, others only at key times like her birthday or New Year and I have depended on school log books, census returns, newspaper articles and circumstantial evidence to fill in some of the gaps. I have interfered as little as possible with Grace's text and then only where the meaning was unclear.

I am a Dexter through my paternal grandmother, Grace Banham Dexter, a daughter of Walter John Dexter (1846-1925), Grace Jane's cousin. I have mentioned that the family was a literary one; they were also highly artistic. In each generation were artists, painters, lace designers and even a cartoonist, Dudley Watkins. Generations of artisans, strong in the Baptist persuasion and believers in self-education and a social Gospel, influenced Grace and continue to throw up writers and artists (and preachers!) in succeeding generations. My research has caused me to discover 'new' cousins in America, Australia, Spain and many parts of Britain — and they are still emerging! The research is by no means complete, so if you can help, I would be delighted to hear from you. My address may be found on the inside title page of this volume.

Rowena Edlin-White, 2005

Grace's Diary

Letter enclosed with the journal to Mrs Joyce Rutt née Rest

Bella Vista
South Stoke
Bath

16.3.57

My dear cousin Joyce,

I was so pleased to receive your letter and to know that you take such an interest in the social activities of your church — as do so many in Manver's St, where I now attend on Sunday mornings — my age preventing me from helping in scarcely more than this; but when Mr Darvill called to see me once I told him of the interview I had when I was 20 with Miss Nightingale and he was so much interested as to ask me to give a short account at one of their socials, so, eventually, I learned the piece of poetry she so beautifully read to me and, though I had to stop twice to remember the words I finished it, and told them a little of my visit to her house.

Now, dear, it would take me a long time to write all about it — so I'm sending you a journal I kept of my doings during those years and what I wrote about Florence Nightingale is exactly what I have always remembered. One thing other than is in the account and which I think, gives the truth to her kind feelings for people is this: I had to defer, for a week, going to see her — owing to a swollen face — through toothache, so, after the tea I had in a small room — of a dainty mutton chop and delicious sweet (I often wondered what was in it!) I was conducted upstairs and as soon as the door — to a long room, was opened I heard a voice saying — "And how's that poor face?" There are the very words. Didn't they show real sympathy and this even before I saw her face! I had the latest "Life" of her by Mrs Cecil Woodham-Smith given to me a year last Christmas and was overwhelmed by the work of many kinds, she had to do in order to get what she knew was needed done — fighting as it were, with War Office authorities involving illness at times, yet continuing resolute until things were accomplished. Truly, she was one of the Greatest benefactors in Our History as a Nation! Well, it was indeed a

4

great event in my life then. I stayed with Mrs Godfrey Lushington whose husband was a Secretary of State under Queen Victoria and she was one of the nicest people I ever met and went up a ladder in the library to get a book for me to read (though I never even looked at it. I was in London for the 1st time)! and lighted the fire in my bedroom which was in Birdcage Walk, St James' Park. She asked where I would like to go and sent 2 hospital nurses with me to Westminster Abbey, and after lunch she took me to Miss Nightingale's in a carriage and pair with coach and footmen — that was unique to me! The rest you will see on the pages where I've put papers to mark them. There's a lovely letter from her which I copied and you will see it in the journal, also one from Mrs Lushington written after having had to leave the school. It is kindness indeed. Now, dear I'm a bit tired so will only say that I wish you success and hope your talk will interest and please all who listen. Every good wish to your dear husband, your father and yourself. With love to each

Always your affectionate Cousin,

Grace

P. S. You will perhaps see a few things on other pages than those marked telling of my life at that period. One, I noticed, said, "I'm getting £40 a year now so shall be able to keep myself entirely." Unbelievable today! Yet we were happy and more contented with good food, nice clothes and good friends. I never remember hearing anyone complain of her salary being too low. We just took it and were glad when it was increased. That's all. You can keep this book if you would like to do so.

✦1884✦

**Grace is eighteen when she begins her Diary. The family are living at
1, Burton Street, Sherwood, a suburb of Nottingham. On the inside cover
of the Diary she notes that she "commenced teaching Jinny and Beaty on
Wednesday July 24 1883". Beaty was her niece; the identity of Jinny is
unknown.**

Feby. 2nd
I have resolved today to begin to write this journal, and to express my
thoughts and feelings in it which I have longed to do for some time. I will
begin with a short sketch of my life.

I was born on Sept. 15 1865. My parents were at that time very poor, but
as I grew older our circumstances altered for the better, and we lived
comfortably though not in affluence. My childhood was a very happy one
although our home was not what it might have been. I mean that it was not
always peaceable. But I had plenty of play and my parents were indulgent
(at least my Mother was) as I was the youngest child. I have one sister &
brother. The former being 13 years older than I & the latter 10. When I was
about 13 years of age we had an Italian gentleman come to live with us. He
was very courteous and kind, but I had a peculiar aversion to him for which
I am now very sorry. But although I was so unkind and rude to him, he
liked me very much. It was a very pleasant time when he lived with us. He
used to come home in the evening & tell us tales of Italy and other places
where he had been. I often think of it now and wish they could come over
again. Oh! how differently I should act. But he is in France now, I
suppose, though we have not heard from him for a long time. He has been
to see us twice since he left. A little while after that our circumstances
changed and we were obliged to leave our comfortable home and go to live
in a small house with a shop. I was just turned fourteen, and thought I
should like to do something for my own living, so I decided to be a teacher. I
went, but found it very difficult for some time, as I had never been in a
public school in my life before[1]. The children were often unruly and I was
young and had not the control over them as I had afterwards. I was a
teacher for three years and progressed very well in my learning. I also

---

[1]   It is very probable that Grace was educated at home by her parents.

became a good teacher, but had to leave on account of my health which was at that time very poor through over study and hard work in the school[2]. I was very sorry to give it up but the doctor said I must if I wished to have my life, which of course I did for a little while longer at any rate. During these three years we had a deal of trouble. My brother who was married lost his wife & dear little baby, Ethel Grace. Poor Maria, she was so dear to us through her illness (which was consumption). She was so patient and forbearing. How her illness was the perfecting of her faith! Before that she was very quick tempered, though amiable and pleasant to live with. But she afterwards became "perfect through suffering." All her former faults left her and she was loving and gentle to us all. How sweet it is to recall her dear face, and think of her, how she always had a smile of welcome for us when we went to see her, and spoke so cheerfully, saying always that she was ready to go when the Lord thought fit to take her. I was the only one of the family there with her when she died. Oh! how happily she died. She longed to go to be with her Saviour. She asked me to sing to her, "I heard the voice of Jesus say etc."[3], but I could not at first, owing to my grief. I conquered it after a little while, & sang to her. How shall I ever forget the look she gave me when she said "thank you"? We sat up with her some time watching, then she would make me go & lie down. I went, but was soon called to see her take her last breath. Oh! how peacefully she passed away just like a little child going to sleep. She took three long breaths & then her spirit had winged its flight to "fairer realms on high." She died at Trowell, Notts. May 21st 1882. Aged 24 years. It is sad that one so young & beautiful should be snatched from us, but it was our Father's will. Dear little Ethel was six months old when she died. She left us before her Mother about seventeen months. She was a sweet angelic little child, and died of Bronchitis.

I was baptised in those three years. I gave myself to Christ, was buried with Him in baptism, & rose to newness of life. But have I indeed walked in newness of life? Have I indeed crucified the flesh & not walked in the lusts thereof? I am afraid not. Oh! when I look back to my past life & see how little I have done for Him Who has done so much for me, I am filled with shame and repentance. I have determined by the help of Christ to start afresh from this time, & try to follow more closely in the footsteps of my Lord and Master. I think I was never truly converted. I thought I was,

---

2 Sneinton Board School, Notintone St, Nottingham; until 1876 the Albion Sabbath Schools.
3 By Horatius Bonar, 1846.

feeling happy for the time being, but how thoughtless I have been; giving way to sinful thoughts, to pride, arrogance, self-conceit, evil tempers, and many other things which are horrible in the sight of Him, "Who is too pure to behold iniquity." May the Lord help me to keep to the good resolution I have formed. This last year we have had another very great trouble, it seems as if there was nothing else for us, to bring us to the Saviour and keep us in the narrow path. But we are not there now, our home is not what it should be, there is too much strife & ill feeling to one another. We are not kind & long suffering, not self sacrificing to each other. We want to have our own way instead of yielding to each other. I hope my striving to do right will influence all. I have a very strong spirit, I know I am not obliging, but I will try to be so. I am proud, but I will try to conquer it by God's help. I said we have had a great trouble during the last year, it was the loss of another of my Brother's dear little ones, our Darling Hilda. How can I write about her, it almost breaks my heart to think of her. She was born about five months before Dear Maria died. We brought her to our house & nursed and cared for her till she was fifteen months old, then she was taken from us. This was another chastisement almost heavier than the other two and yet we seem to have profited very little by it. Surely we shall do, before the Lord stretches out his hand again on us. That dear child, she was like an angel sent from Heaven to us, but the Lord thought fit to take her away again because we were so sinful. When I think of her sweet little ways, of how she learned to love us & say things in her baby way, it makes my heart bleed, to think, that she had to be taken away, she was so very beautiful; with her lovely little face, with its rosy cheeks, & blue eyes, that looked from under long eyelashes that swept her cheeks, when she closed them. Her clearly defined nose & lovely mouth & dimpled chin, were matchless. Everyone said "How lovely she is." Now she is an angel of light beholding the face of her Father in Heaven. May we live so that we may soon join her. Our Darling's death made a deeper impression on me than anything else in my life. I loved her so. I often said when she was alive & well that I thought I should die if she did. Now I feel that I should not fear death if I were prepared to go because it would take me to her, it is another link to Heaven. But, if I have to live, I hope I shall lead a useful life, doing all the good I can and trying to live a Christian life.

It is Sunday afternoon (I began to write this last night) everything is so peaceful. I have tried today to live a better life. I have been so happy in trying & hope I shall continue in well doing. It is the ordinance[4] tonight. I don't know whether I shall go. If I do I hope I shall not be distracted with other thoughts but have my mind fixed on my Saviour. What a terrible thing it is to eat and drink of that sacred emblem unworthily. "Wherefore whosoever shall eat this bread, and drink this cup of the Lord unworthily, shall be guilty of the body & blood of the Lord." [1]Cor. XI. 27.

Sunday Night Feb. 3rd

I have been to Chapel[5]. We have had a good time. I feel so happy tonight having tried to live for others instead of myself today. I hope I shall continue to do so tomorrow & forever. How delightful it is to remember the death of Our Lord, when we know it purchased for us life everlasting. What wondrous love that was that made Him suffer for our iniquities. O that we may love Him more and serve Him better than we have done.

Feby. 6th

I have been reading a book entitled, "Stepping Heavenward".[6] It is written in the form of a journal describing the life of a girl who was very faulty in many things. Her chief sin was a hasty temper, which was always leading her to do and say things, of which she afterwards repented. It shows how by constant prayer and watchfulness she overcame it at last, though after many years. I enjoyed reading the book very much. It did not begin with a perfect character (which is often the case in books), but with one that was always falling into temptation (just as I am) and some times almost giving up in despair of ever being better; but somehow she always manages to rise again through conversations with kind religious friends, & prayer to God to give her the victory over sin. She at last becomes a perfect character (so far at least as we can be in this world), her life being entirely in harmony with that of her Master. All her quick temper leaves her and she is loving and gentle as a child. She goes through much suffering and affliction before attaining that perfection of character, loses several dear friends — is poor — her bodily strength leaves her & she is an invalid for years so that after all that, she is refined and made like unto pure gold. I wonder sometimes if ever I shall be like her, what discipline she had to endure. Shall I have to suffer

---

4   Eucharistic service.
5   Stoney St Chapel (Baptist) in the Lace Market, Nottingham.
6   *Stepping Heavenwards* by American author Elizabeth Prentiss (1818-1878) 1st pub. 1869.

the same? Perhaps so. It takes a great deal to break this stubborn will of ours and to mould it & fashion it like unto the Divine One. I have not been so happy since Sunday. I have fallen into so many sins since then. Although I have conquered through Jesus more than in previous efforts, I am not self-sacrificing enough, but want too much of my own way. I am very weak too, in being able to resist temptation — seem so easily drawn aside — have not strength of character enough — am proud. How dreadful it is to write these things down, to see what one is in black and white, but if it makes me better with self-examination I don't care. There is one temptation which I pray God to take from me & help me to overcome. I have prayed many times but it is not conquered yet. I hope it will be in time. It is very great. I am all alone this afternoon. Mother is out and Beaty is at play. Dear little Beaty, how I love her; but I am not kind enough to her. I often speak very sharp to her and am not gentle with her over her lessons. She has no Mamma & no sisters only her dear Papa; how I ought to love & be kind to this lonely little one.

March 2nd Sunday Night
All are out but Beaty & Me. She is gone to bed and I am just going to write a little more in this book. It is nearly a month since I wrote in it before. I don't seem to have lived much better during that time. I have tried but fail so often. There is one thing that I can do, now, though, that I could not do before, that is, I can go when I have sinned and pour out my soul to God in prayer and feel that He loves and cares for me & forgives me & will strengthen me when I ask Him. I am sure there is great power in prayer. I have never felt it so much as lately. I used to be often very abstracted when praying, but I can now fix my thoughts more on my Saviour and not let other things be mixed with them. I have asked the Lord to give me this concentration of thought on Himself & I believe He has. On St Valentine's Day, my dear sister Mary gave me a beautiful silver brooch, another token of her affection for me. I have tried to be kinder to her since then than I was before. I know I do not submit to her as I should; she being the older sister, I have such a proud spirit (I am ashamed to confess) but I am trying to be different. I do love her very much and know that if she has a quick temper and is rather exacting as I think, she is good at heart and can always be won with love. I think she would do anything for anyone she loved. I have got a card to collect £2.2 for the Chapels, before Easter, so I must go tomorrow

and try what I can get from my friends. I hope I shall be able to make it all up by the time. I think I shall.

❧ 1885 ❧

Tragedy continued to afflict the family, including the death of Aunt Jane's daughter Sarah, who died of puerperal fever following childbirth, leaving three little girls, Joyce, Mabel and Sarah. Their father, Philip Weigel, a German cabinet-maker, left Nottingham for America to try to earn enough to support his family, but died of TB in 1897[7]. Jane Dawkins, who was 70 at the time of Sarah's death, brought up the three girls herself.

Grace's family moved across town to Radford where her father was manager for J. S. Wells, a hosiery manufacturer.

Feby 23rd 1885

It is nearly a year since I last wrote in this book. Many events have transpired since that time. Amongst other things I have lost several dear friends. My dear Uncle Walter[8] has died, also my cousin Sarah Weigel[9], and my dear friend May Meldrum besides others with whom I was well acquainted. It has been a very sad year to us all. Dear Cousin Sarah was in the full bloom of womanhood when she was cut off so suddenly without scarcely a moment's notice; as also was our other dear friend, she being only twenty-two [MM, not SW]. It seems impossible to realise that they are gone, but we have no doubt that there is an unseen Hand working mysteriously for our good, although we cannot understand the reason always at the time.

My brother John has married again in the last year.[10] May the blessing of health rest on the union. They live at Beeston, Notts. We have left Sherwood & now reside in Player St, Alfreton Rd.[11] where I am at present keeping a private school. I have seven children now but am hoping to have more as the Spring advances.

---

[7] The letters of Philip Weigel, 1890-97 are in the Nottinghamshire Archives.
[8] Walter Dexter (1821-84), elder brother to Grace's father John. Died 26th July 1884, aged 63.
[9] Sarah Young Weigel (1858-84). Died 9th July 1884, aged 27.
[10] To Clara Redmill at Holy Trinity Church, Nottingham, on 23rd Oct. 1884.
[11] 12 Player St, Radford (now demolished).

We have now united ourselves with the friends at Prospect Place, Radford owing to the distance to Stoney St. Chapel which was so great. It was a trial to us to leave S. St. especially to me as I was baptised there. It was like leaving my home where I first learned to love & follow Christ to go among strangers. The Brethren were also sorry to part with us; but I think we shall be very happy where we are. They are so cordial and warm-hearted, and have welcomed us to their fellowship with such brotherly love.[12] I am able to teach in the school here which it was not possible for me to do at S. St. My Father has the first class of boys. I have the second class of girls. My great desire & fervent prayer is that I may be able to instruct them in all truth & righteousness, and that God will shower down upon them & upon me His best gifts & grace & endue our hearts with wisdom & understanding. I believe He will. Had a very happy day yesterday it being Sunday. Visited some of my friends at Sherwood in the afternoon who were very glad to see me, and my dear Mother also went with me. It is so pleasant to go out with her.

Monday 2nd March

Mr Hugues (the gentleman I mentioned at the beginning of this journal) was here yesterday. We had a very pleasant evening. My brother and his wife were also with us. We did not go to Chapel because Mr H. was here in the evening. I am sorry for that. We had such a comforting discourse in the morning, the text was "My presence shall go with thee & I will give thee rest" Ex. XXXIII.14.

I have a very full class on Sunday morning; I begin to like the girls very much. Was very tired on Sunday morning and felt as if I could scarcely rouse myself to go, having a severe headache, but I went and was rewarded with seeing so many of them. What a pity it would have been had they had no teacher.

Mr H. is coming for tea this afternoon. I wish the eyes of his understanding were opened so that he could see the beauty of true religion; I pray that the Lord will reveal himself to him ere long.

---

12   Prospect Place Chapel already had family connections - 'Uncle Walter' and family had lived nearby and worshipped there, and at this time his son, Walter John Dexter , was organist.

Sunday March 8th

Mr H. went away on Thursday morning, he came to see us several times & brought some beautiful flowers. He came in to my school to see it before he went.

We had a <u>Cottage Meeting</u> in our parlour this afternoon. About twenty friends came. We had singing & prayer. Then one friend read from Isaiah, "He was despised & rejected". My Father spoke a few words on the chapter afterwards to the young people who were present. Then one or two related their experience; how they were once wanderers in the broad way but had now obtained forgiveness through our Lord Jesus Christ.

It is the ordinance of the Lord's Supper tonight. I hope we shall be blest & able to start afresh on our Christian way after we have partaken of the emblems which remind us of the great sacrifice offered once for all.

Monday March 15th

I went to Stoney St. Chapel last night to hear Mr Griffiths[13] preach. I shall not be able to hear him many more times as he is going to leave S.S. He is going to London I suppose & intends taking to the bar. I enjoyed his sermon very much, the subject was the "Christian Race" (Cor. 1. IX 24 to 27 verses). He fully described the Olympian Sports. One of the chief features of them was equality. So long as they were of Grecian birth & free & adhered to the rules, then the Prince & Peasant were on the same level in these games. They stood side by side and both had a chance of winning the same prize. He said <u>they</u> were temperate in all things. And if they could adhere to these restrictions in order to win a corruptible crown, how much more should <u>we</u> strive to bring our bodies into subjection as the Apostle says in the last verse to win an incorruptible one — lest by any means we should be call *(sic)* away.

He described the honours that were bestowed upon the victor, not in silver & gold but what he valued more highly, the esteem & respect of the people. When he returned from the sports to his own town, he was greeted with triumphant arches, a banquet was prepared for him, and he occupied the highest place at the ceremony. If there were other sports in that locality he again commanded the first seat. If in battle he fought for his country he had the most honoured place in fighting which was at the King's side. He said

---

[13]   Rev. R. F. Griffiths was Minister of Stoney Street and Barker Gate Chapels.

the Apostle Paul would have ridiculed the idea of any one starting to run a race if he had no intention of gaining the goal. They all started fully intending to win, but many failed. There was only one crown in those games. One man only won the laurels. But in our race many will win, and when we reach the heavenly goal there will be many crowns — not perishable as they were, lasting but a few hours without drooping — but everlasting. "A crown of life which shall never fade."

I enjoyed it so much and yet it made me feel sad. I know I am in the Christian race but whether I shall win or not I sometimes doubt. He spoke "of the success not being diverted by anything around them, of the acclamation of the people or any other thing, but having their minds & energies fixed on one thing — Winning." Now my heart I feel is not fixed in one sense, it wanders so often to things around. I cannot realise that Christ is my all in all and that whatever happens to me whether I am rich or poor, ill or well or whatever state I am it matters not so long as He is with me. I am so ambitious, want to be more than I am. This enchains my thought more than Christ. I heard two sermons on nearly the same subject yesterday. The morning sermon was on the equipment necessary for the Christian warfare, Ephesians VI. I wish I could fight as a true soldier. But I will not give up. I feel that my Saviour loves me and will help me through, and when I fall, if I pray to Him He will be near and help me. I have many trials which I could not mention: God only knows. Oh! that I may go through the fight and run the race and at last come out more than conqueror through Him who loved me. If we could only think & realise it, we should not mind the difficulties which we have to encounter here; but should look forward to the recompense of the reward. May God help me.

Sunday March 22nd

All are gone to Chapel. I am prevented through a severe cold. We must suffer disappointments sometimes. It has been one to me today. My class at the Sunday School has been neglected, and I have missed the services of the Lord's house. All through some inadvertence on my part perhaps. They say I am so careless in not taking care of myself. I must try to alter in this respect too.

My Father presented me with a volume of Mr E. Young's Night Thoughts yesterday. I have read a little of it. And what I have read I have not yet thoroughly digested. One of his great complaints seems to be the loss of

14

Time. Wasted, unimproved time. In Night 1st he says "We take no note of time But from its loss. To give it then a tongue Is wise in man. As if an angel spoke, I feel the solemn sound. If heard aright, It is the knell of my departed hours. Where are they? With the years beyond the flood."[14]
Again in Night II,
"Each night we die;
Each morn are born anew: each day a life!
And shall we kill each day? If trifling kills,
Sure vice must butcher. O what heaps of slain
Cry out for very vengeance on us! Time destroy'd
Is suicide, where more than blood is split:
Time flies, death urges, knells call, Heaven invites,
Hell threatens: all exerts; in effort all,
More than creation, labours! — Labours more?
And is there in creation, what, amidst
This tumult universal, wing'd dispatch,
And ardent energy, supinely yawns? —
Man sleeps, and man alone; and man, whose fate,
Fate irreversible, entire, extreme,
Endless, hair-hung, breeze-shaken, o'er the gulf
A moment trembles; drops! and man, for whom
All else is in alarm; man, the sole cause
Of this surrounding storm! and yet he sleeps,
As the storm rock'd to rest!—Throw years away?
Throw empires, and be blameless:"[15]

I want some knowledge. I feel so ignorant, and, more, I know I am. O! for perseverance to gain knowledge and understanding. I waste my time. I do not husband every moment; and utilise every hour. I am striving to perfect myself in French but I do not know whether I shall be energetic enough to persevere, and master all the difficulties.

My Father was reading a short account of the life of Margaret Fuller[16] the other day. She was very learned, but she did not gain her knowledge by longing for it. She rose at five every morning to study. Labouring for the

---

[14] *The Poetical Works of Edward Young*, pub. Milner & Sowerby pp 2-3.
[15] *op cit* pp 21-22.
[16] Margaret Fuller Ossoli, American author, 1810-1850.

most part under adverse circumstances but she was so indefatigable that she at last reaped the fruit of her exertions. Oh! that I had this indomitable will, this fixed purpose. I am going to strive to rise early and try to succeed. It is no use giving in. I will write down every week how I succeed. I am so glad I began to write in this book. I feel that when I write down here anything which I plan to do, it is sacred and must be fulfilled. I have so many slips in my Christian life. When "I would do good evil is present with me." I am so ungrateful to my dear Mother; and she is so good to me. She asked for something of mine this morning, something so trifling, and I objected to giving it her. Afterwards I was so grieved that I had for a moment demurred and asked her to forgive me. She is such a kind dear Mother, so self sacrificing, that if I could give all that I have or do anything it would not in the least recompense her for all her manifold kindness. The very least I can do is to be obliging and loving to her. I pray to the Lord that he will not allow Satan to enter my heart to tempt me to wrong.

In June the family moved to Robin Hood, a tiny hamlet on the canal beside Whatstandwell, a few miles from Matlock, so that John Dexter could work at Wharmby's Mills. From her description, it appears they occupied the house called Oakford Cottage on Robin Hood Rd. From here Grace could walk the two miles or so to Lea School.

July 18th
Another change. Here we are at Whatstandwell, Derbyshire. We have left Nottm. with all its old associations for a new abode. Who would have dreamt last year that we should be here? Father has come to Mr Wharmby's Mill[17], and so it happens that we are all stationed here for the present, except Mary & John who are still at N[ottingham] & Beeston. Mary is come to stay a week with us. We have been here 6 weeks. It seems so long. The greatest trouble to me at leaving N. was the giving up of my day school & Sunday School. But so it is we must not consider this life as our place of rest. We are journeying on & must bear with the changes & breakings up of our plans. We are very much delighted with this place at present. It being the middle of summer everything looks lovely. Everything is clothed with nature's beauteous garb. From my window as I write the hills rise (to my mind) one height above another clothed with luxuriant trees & vegetation.

---

[17] Samuel Wharmby's Saw Mills, Robin Hood Mill, Whatstandwell (Kelly's Trade Dir. 1887)

Things are so prolific, growth springing up out of unlikely places. I can also see the canal, Derwent & railway (which runs close by) & beautiful green fields. How enchanting it is. So different to the closed-up house we lived in at N. The house is huge so we like it very much. We can see the hand of God in all this. He has provided again for our necessities. Continually we are the recipients of His bounty. I grieve not at leaving the town of my birth, save for the before mentioned reasons. I feel that the Lord is guiding me, that He knows what is best. I know not what may be my future but have full confidence in Him to lead me aright. I am trying to get a situation in a school.

Sept 15/ 85

My birthday! I am twenty today. I am engaged at Lea School, for the present.[18] My great desire is to strive to inculcate high and right principles into the children. Trust I shall succeed. Hope all things. Nil desperandum!

Dec 16th 1885

I have been at Lea School nearly four months now. How soon the timer has gone. I should have gone to London to see Miss Florence Nightingale & Mrs G. Lushington as yesterday, but am prevented by a severe cold, with neuralgia. I am getting better now. The acute pain has gone and I trust to be able to travel on Friday 18th. The workings of providence are stranger to me now than ever. Why are we brought here? I am persuaded the hand of God is in it all, working for our good. We shall yet praise Him. The lady of whom I have thought in my childhood, as being the embodiment of all noble self sacrifice & goodness — Miss Nightingale, I am actually going to see & speak with. It is all so strange & mystic now, but will be clearer by & by. I have never been to London before, all will be new to me. I do not expect to see much of the city as I shall be back in a day or two. The children at school are giving the entertainment tonight from which I am debarred by my indisposition. I teach the fourth standard at present. I am endeavouring to the best of my ability to educate them in feelings of gentleness & the Christian courtesy. I do not find the disposition of country children so generous as that of those in the town. There is always a great desire for the most advantageous place, no giving way one to another, which fault will

---

[18]   Grace was appointed on 7th September 1885.

take I fear a deal of uprooting. Still we must hope all things. "Only be strong and of good courage." I take more interest in teaching now than ever feeling that whatsoever my hand hath found to do I will do it with all my might. My dear Mother & Father have been & are so kind to me & shewing such anxiety for my well being. Will it ever be in my power in any measure to show my deep love for them? I trust it may.

Lea School was local to Lea Hurst, Florence Nightingale's family home, and she took a keen interest in it. Mrs Lushington was Treasurer of the Board of Governors. The Log Book[19] gives some indication of the difficulties under which the teaching staff laboured: irregular attendance due to seasonal agricultural work, disease and lack of interest on the part of parents. Discipline was harsh, both girls and boys being caned liberally, and this was one aspect of the job Grace found impossible to administer.
  Grace's visit to see Florence Nightingale in London was probably the most formative event of her young life. Miss Nightingale summoned her in order to access her suitability to remain at Lea School after her probationary period. She took a keen interest in the young trainee teachers at Lea, and in spite of Grace's failure to cope, continued to correspond with her and encourage her in her career for some years.

❧1886☙

Jany 24 Sunday
  Since I last wrote I have been to London to see Miss Nightingale & Mrs Lushington[20]. It is impossible for me to write all I saw & felt while there but just a few things I will mention. I was not well on starting having been suffering from neuralgia all week. It was Friday. On arriving at St Pancras I took a cab & proceeded to Mrs Lushington's. When there I was treated very kindly by her. Had a very nice & comfortable bedroom with a fire. After dinner went with a maidservant to Westminster Abbey (Mrs L. lives close to). Service was going on. A strange feeling came over me. Was it reality that I stood in that edifice of which I had heard & read so much, with its historic renown? The singing was beautiful coming from the far end of the Abbey resounding along the vaulted roof. I had not an opportunity of

19 Log Book of Lea School 1862-1888.
20 According to the Log Book she was away in London 18-21 Dec. 1885

reading the inscriptions on the tombs as (being winter) it is closed early. But I shall never forget the calm that came over my spirit while there, in the presence, as it were, of the mighty dead, I thought of some of their lives, some active, ambitious, great geniuses yet there is an end of all things & their end came as will ours. I am more & more convinced that in this life our sole aim & object should be to do the will of God. It is greater by far to please Him & to bend our whole thought thereto, than to be ambitious for anything else. These men, many of them had an idea before them whether in religion, in war, in art, in science, in literature, in philanthropy, in politics, or whatsoever thing they bent their minds. They accomplished their desire by singleness of purpose & died, leaving the fruits of their labour for the benefit of mankind. We shall die too. O! may we do something though but in a small measure to leave the world better for our being. I went on leaving the Abbey past the Houses of Parliament on to Westminster Bridge then back to Mrs Lushington's.

At 4.30 I went with Mrs L. in the carriage to Miss Nightingale's (by the by I may say here that I had never been in a carriage & pair before with footman & coachman so I am afraid I was a little vain of the honour of so doing) where we had a dainty tea before seeing Miss N. How am I to describe her? I had not formed a very favourable impression of her appearance by report; but found her a lady most charmante. Such a beautiful, subdued face & voice. She talked to me so easily & pleasantly that I was not constrained in my own manner but felt that I could speak to her as freely as possible. I believe her to be a true Christian lady by her conversation with me. She said she had been intimately acquainted with General Gordon. She spoke of him as being a man, whose whole life was consecrated & said that on his entering the room you felt his presence as being that of a holy & upright man. A picture hanging before us turned the subject to that of the Crimean War. Miss Nightingale then read me a poem by Tennyson on "The Charge of the Light Brigade". She read it with great expression, every phase of their movement being portrayed by the inflections of her voice. I think the interview was — taking it as a whole — the most pleasant I have ever spent in my life, interspersed as it was by these (to me) delightful references. I stayed all night at Mrs L's & went next day (Sat) to the Dore Gallery in New Bond St. Mrs Lushington kindly sent for two hospital nurses to accompany me. They were very nice companions. I cannot in my humble opinion but endorse the opinion of the press that his great picture "Christ Leaving the Praetorium"[21] was nothing short of an inspiration. I never saw so impressive a picture before. The sublimity & dignity of Our Lord contrasts the most vividly with the expression of countenance of the Chief Priests & Scribes together with those of the multitude. A more heterogeneous assemblage it would I think be difficult to conceive on canvas. Several other pictures of great merit claimed my attention of which I cannot write because of their number. I went inside Westminster Hospital, through several wards. Everything was so cheerful & clean.

On leaving Mrs Lushington I went in a cab to Bow where I stayed with Mrs Rhodes til Monday. I had an opportunity by this means of seeing East & West London. A great disparity truly. On Sunday visited St Paul's. I had heard it was a very large Cathedral but could not have conceived its being so large as I found it. I was astounded. What an immense concourse of people it must hold when full! Mr & Mrs Rhodes & family were very kind to me as was everybody. On Monday I came back starting at 12 o'clock. So ended my visit to the Great Metropolis. It has fully realised my expectations even exceeded them. I have the greatest pleasure in looking back on that event in my life. Now it is settled that I stay at the School till I have sat for my scholarship examination. After then fresh arrangements will be made. This poem of Cowper's is I think beautifully appropriate to my reflections on entering Westminster Abbey.

"Martyrs"

Patriots have toil'd, & in their country's cause
Bled nobly; & their deeds, as they deserve,
Receive proud recompense. We give in charge
Their names to the sweet lyre. Th' historic muse,
Proud of the treasure, marches with it down
To latest times; and Sculpture, in her turn,
Gives bond in stone, & ever-during brass
To guard them, and to immortalize her trust:
But fairer wreathes are due, though never paid,
To those, who, posted at the shrine of Truth,
Have fallen in her defence. A patriot's blood,
Well spent in such a strife, may earn indeed,

---

[21]   By Gustave Dore, 1832-83.

And for a time ensure, to his lov'd land
The sweets of liberty and equal laws;
But martyrs struggle for a brighter prize,
And win it with more pain. Their blood is shed
In confirmation of the noblest claim —
Our claim to feed upon immortal truth,
To walk with God, to be divinely free,
To soar, and to anticipate the skies.
Let few remember them. They lived unknown
Till persecution dragg'd them into fame,
And chased them up to heaven. Their ashes flew
— No marble tells us whither. With their names
No bard embalms & sanctifies his song:
And history, so warm in meaner themes,
Is cold on this. She execrates indeed
The tyranny, that doom'd them to the fire,
But gives the glorious sufferers little praise.[22]

Extract from Lea School Log Book, 19 February 1886:
"Spoke to Miss Dexter about her class. The discipline has been very lax of late and the last week has been bad. Order is not maintained and there is great want of attention to the work on the part of the children, boys especially."
Again, on 24th February:
"Miss Dexter's class is still in unsatisfactory state of discipline..."

March 6th
We are having very severe weather. Snow on the ground several inches thick. Has been snowing all week. Trade is extremely depressed, thousands out of employment all over the country[23]. What will the poor things do who cannot get the necessaries of life at this inclement season? Funds for the relief of the poor have been started in London & other large towns. Why do not the rich deny themselves of the greater part of their luxuries to aid the destitute? Father read of the grand reception held by the Queen yesterday, how the ladies were all dressed so richly & adorned with costly ornaments &

---

[22]   William Cowper, from *The Task*, Book V, 1785.
[23]   It was this severe slump in trade which forced cousin Sarah's widower, Philip Weigel, to leave Nottingham for America, in order to provide for his children.

jewels. If they had instead of appearing at this time in such gorgeous apparel, gone plainly dressed visiting & relieving the distressed it seems to me they would have pleased the Divine master more who said to the young man having great possessions, "Go sell all that thou hast & give to the poor & thou shalt have treasure in Heaven." Perhaps if I were rich I should cling as much or more than they do to this world's goods, but I feel now that if I had wealth I should employ it in helping & succouring those who are cold & destitute. Riots have been in London & elsewhere. Men starving for want of food. Rich men have given — it is true — out of their abundance, but still there is the "Battle Cry", no work! no work! We must trust & pray that relief may soon come to them in the shape of a revival in trade, which is what they want — they do not desire charity but employment, but when the latter cannot be had, it is the duty of those who want for nothing to open their hearts & hands & give freely as the Lord has prospered & given to them.

Grace had several bouts of ill-health during the month of March, probably exacerbated by her problems at school. When she returned to work on 29th March, the entry in the Log Book states: "Miss Dexter, who is still looking very unwell, resumed duties this afternoon."

March 29
O weariness, ill again. Three days last week I was away from school. Could not go this (Monday) morning. Am going to try this afternoon.

Extract from Lea School Log Book, 13 April 1886:
"Since the entry on Feb 24, have pointed out several times to Miss Dexter that the state of her class is most unsatisfactory as regards the discipline... I have frequently told Miss Dexter to insist on order, before teaching, but she continues her teaching if only a few are attentive notwithstanding that a number of children may be conversing on subjects foreign to the lesson."

May 24
I am greatly discouraged in teaching. The children are so unruly. Today has been a hard day. 16 boys to teach & 11 girls. I have written to Miss Nightingale at her request to tell her how I get on. I told her everything. She has not replied yet. I do not know what she thinks. She sent me two

beautiful engravings, "Christ the Light of the World", "Christ the Good Shepherd" & wrote me such a kind letter. Hope I shall not have to leave yet although I have so much to try me. O, what am I to do! I want to govern by love & gentleness if I can but it seems impossible. Gave a lesson on "The Monkey" with upper Standards last week. I was so glad they all praised it very much, Mr Butler & the teachers. But now I am depressed again.

By June, Grace had been demoted to being a mere classroom assistant; she became completely demoralised and her engagement was terminated.

July 23rd
My engagement terminated at Lea School June 30th & they have not re-engaged me. Have been to Leicester, from there to Nottingham for my Examination 2.S. Altogether away five weeks. Returned home today. Have written as to a situation as Assistant to the Arnold School Bd. today. I hope something will soon open out for me. Don't feel able to write details respecting anything. Clara & Baby Hilda[24] have come with me. It is a sweet little thing. My dear Mother! I am so glad to have come back to help her; she has been ill. O! If I could help her materially I would be so happy. May the time soon come when I can, bless her & dear Father. They are so kind & self sacrificing.

July 26th
Went yesterday Sunday to Crich in the evening. Afterwards went with my father to visit Mr Hardstone who is ill. It was so refreshing to one's spirit to go & speak with a God fearing Christian man. He spoke of heaven and the ever recurring source of joy which we shall have there. He said "O! the delight of seeing our friends & speaking with them: that will give us supreme delight, but more than that we shall have the company of Jesus "our elder brother", he will be ever with us & then all sorrow & sighs shall be done away" and "God shall wipe away all tears from our eyes. O heaven!" he said, "what dreams of bliss are presented at the very name." While he was ill these thoughts gave him the sweetest consolation. I felt so happy to go & see this good old man. The brethren at Crich[25] are very sympathetic

---

24   John and Clara's daughter Hilda Clarissa Gertrude was born around March/April 1886. It was not unusual to give a child the name of a deceased sibling.
25   Crich Baptist Church which the family attended whilst living at Whatstandwell.

simple Christian people rejoicing with those who rejoice & weeping with those who weep. Feel more & more drawn towards them. This morning (Monday) I have had a letter from Mrs Lushington which I think I will transcribe here.

Great Bedwyn
Hungerford
July 23rd

Dear Miss Dexter
    Thank you for your letter — I am glad to have what I am sure is a true as well as a very kindly expression of your feelings about leaving Lea School. There has never been a doubt as to your earnestness & pains-taking in the performance of your school duties — nor of your kindness & patience with the children & your desire to teach and influence them in the best way — what we have understood is what I now think you yourself feel to be the case, that you are not well able for the work of a mixed school with large classes and rougher noisier boys — such teaching requires besides physical strength, a certain habit of the thing:- which needs to be acquired at the very beginning — you had never taught in a mixed school & your practise during the years that you had discontinued teaching in a Board School, had not been of a kind to make it come easy for you. We believe that you have some of the best qualifications for teaching & sincerely hope that you will get work suitable for you.
    I am, very truly yours,
        Beatrice Lushington.

July 31st
Went to see Lucie Miers — a teacher at Lea School.[26] She is such a nice girl, so are her parents — very kind. We sat on the lawn after tea reading & talking, viz. Lucie & I & her four sisters and brothers. Quite an artistic group we made with our parasols & garden chairs. Afterwards we had music in the drawing room. I sang "The Better Land", and played "Les

---

[26]   The Miers family lived at Chapel House, Lea; they became great friends of Grace's. Lucie Miers worked at Lea school until July 1887.

Cloches du Monmartre" & Lucie played from Mozart's Twelfth Mass. Then to finish up the evening we sang a hymn. Lucie read a psalm, and we all knelt down while Mr Miers offered up a true, earnest beautiful prayer. I felt how delightful it was to be amongst good Christian people.

Aug 1st

Mother's birthday. Had a floral service at Crich. Father gave a short address in the afternoon to children & friends — Chapel full — Good preacher. Flowers looked lovely — I went three times — felt happy all day.

Aug 2nd

Bank Holiday. Went with Mother & Clara & baby to Matlock. Saw four scholars in the Sunday School at Prospect Place Chapel where we attended & Father & I taught in the Sunday School. They were delighted to see me as I was with them.

Aug 3rd

Mrs Knighton (Crich) & her son's wife came for tea — Mother prepared a very good tea. We expected Mr & Mrs Kirk (Crich) but they were prevented from coming. Mrs Knighton Jnr. is a school mistress so that we had a good deal of talk about school work. In the evening went to Crich Chapel to hear a student from Nottm. What a magnificent sermon we had! Father said it was fit to be preached before the Queen. The great purpose of it was that we must be childlike always trusting in the mighty power of God & leaving the results with Him. He educed facts from history to show how little a thing involves the whole after course of a man's life. So great being the change oftentimes wrought by circumstances apparently trivial at the moment. What a treat — to hear a sermon like that sometimes. Father is going to write to Mr Griffiths to see if he will come to preach our Chapel Anniversary sermons. I do not know whether he will come from London here.

Had a letter from Miss Nightingale. Cannot transcribe it — there are four sheets. She speaks of discipline of the mind and manner of life — advises me if I would continue in the teaching profession not to take an absorbing interest in politics or anything that would cause my mind to be diverted from its purpose, viz. dwelling on the best ways of controlling & maintaining the interest & attention of my scholars. It is a very kind faithful letter. Mrs

Clough called to see me on Monday, but I was at Matlock. She is Mrs
Lushington's sister. Was so sorry for being out. Have written to her to say
I will go to Ashover to see her if she wishes. Expect a reply tomorrow.

Aug 7
Have received two letters from Mrs Clough this week — one this morning
in which she arranges for to meet me at Holloway at 3 o'clock on
Wednesday. My sister Mary came yesterday to stay with us a little while.

Aug 10
A letter from Mr Griffiths to Father. Father is not at home so I opened it.
He says he will not be able to come to preach the sermons now, but in
September, perhaps the 12th. He will be able to write definitely respecting
the time next week. He says he will certainly be glad to see us and writes —
" I scarcely identified the 'J. Dexter' till I came to the reference to your wife
& Grace." So he remembered Mother and I. I do hope his arrangement will
suit the church and that we shall be able to wait till he comes. I must take
the letter in Father's absence to Mr Kirk @ Crich.
Afternoon have been this morning to show Mr Kirk the letter of Mr
Griffiths. It poured with rain all the way but I felt glad at heart so that
outward annoyances were trivial to me. Mr K. says the 12th of Sept. will
suit so we can now look forward to the pleasure of seeing and hearing Mr
Griffiths.

Aug 13
Had an interview with Mrs Clough on Wednesday (the 11th). She would
like me to write her definitely what course I shall take in regard to another
situation viz. as to whether I would like to be a nursery governess, or take a
situation as assistant in a Board School or — which I think is impossible —
go to College or Boarding School for 4 years. I said to her that the latter
would — I thought — be impossible as I had never been able to gain
sufficient for my own living, always being dependent on my Father &
Mother, and I could not think — even if they were able — of putting them
to further expense. She seemed desirous of helping me in some way, but she
wished to see me in order to know what I thought & what plans I had in
view. In consequence she said her conversation might seem vague to me but
I think she will write & try to do something in it. She also said Miss

Nightingale would like to know what I intended to do. She said Mr Butler[27] spoke kindly respecting me and gave as the reason of my non success at the school that I was not capable of managing the boys. He thought I might do with girls. Mother wants me to remain at home with her a little while perhaps till I know the result of my exams. Clara & Baby went away this morning. They have been here three weeks altogether. Baby cried so at leaving me when she was in the railway carriage. She is a dear little thing. So pretty & engaging.

Aug 15

Mrs Clough called to see me on Friday; my Mother remained in the room during her stay. She said after thinking it over since Wednesday, she had come to the conclusion that it would in her opinion be better for me to continue in the same kind of teaching as heretofore and would advise me to use all the influence at my disposal — by the kind testimony of friends, in order to procure a good situation. My dear father was speaking this morning about the desire he had — if it could possibly be contrived — for me to go to College, or to boarding school to make a "thorough lady of me", as he says. O! that the way might be opened for such a thing. It would just be the fulfilment of my greatest wishes to be highly educated, but how can I think of my dear parents in their declining years being afresh burdened.

We went to the flower show at Holloway yesterday (Saturday) — saw a many friends amongst them. Miss Finney — the young lady who treated me so kindly last winter when skating — she asked me to go with her to tea and we had a very pleasant evening, music etc. Then I came home at night by train from Matlock Bridge. I was delighted to see her again. She returns to Leek — her home — on Tuesday and will call to see us on her way.

At Chapel, this morning, I was pleasurably surprised, to see Miss Meldrum of Nottm., cousin of dear May. She is staying with Mr & Mrs Dawes & will come to see us one day next week. She told me she has never recovered from the shock of poor May's death, they were both about of an age and companions. I remember them coming to our house not long before May died. Two such nice, sweet girls. She returns on Thursday. I am sorry her visit is not longer. Am going to Chapel with Mother & Beaty tonight — Father is at school. Mary gone to Mrs Wheeldon's for the day.

---

27   The Headmaster at Lea School.

Aug 16

Received by post this morning "A Short History of the English People"[28]
by Green from Mrs Clough I presume. I have written to thank her for it.
She spoke of it on Friday and advised me study a certain period — as for an
examination. I shall endeavour to do so. I think it to be a very good history
of the people of this country and one which I shall have great pleasure in
studying.

Aug 21

Wrote yesterday to Miss Nightingale explaining to the best of my ability
the discipline of mind & mode of life to which I subjected myself when at
Lea School in order to further my aim of becoming a successful teacher.
Have had a very severe cold on my chest this week — cannot go out. Mr
Griffiths is coming to us on 12th Septr. Father had another letter from him
this week.

Aug 27

Mary & Beatie[29] went to Nottingham yesterday. We are all alone now,
Father, Mother & I, nevertheless we enjoy the quiet after having had
company nearly all the summer. I think I shall stay at home to help Mother
a month or two, but in the meantime intend to write to Mr Packer & ask him
if he can give me an engagement under the Nottm. Board.

It grieves me to think of going from my dear Mother but we are too poor
for me to stay always with her.

Sept 2nd

I had a letter from my cousin Mrs Richardson[30] yesterday which gave me
great pleasure, they are at Skegness; also one this morning from Mrs &
Miss Clough. Mrs Clough writes as follows:

---

28   John Richard Green, 1874.
29   Beaty seems always to have lived with her grandparents or sometimes with Mary, after her
mother's death, rather than in her father's household. In the 1901 Census, she is found acting
as housekeeper to her grandparents in Duffield.
30   Elizabeth Richardson, nee Dawkins, married William Richardson a boot and shoe
manufacturer in Leicester. It was to their relatively wealthy household that various members
of the family, Grace included, repaired for rest and recuperation at times.

Embley
Rowsley
Aug 31 '86

Dear Miss Dexter,

I think perhaps the enclosed note from my daughter may be some use to you in your study & I am sure she will be very glad to look over or advise in any way she can. I hope you will keep the Green's History & find it useful. If you want more books later on, perhaps it will be possible to find a library to subscribe to unless you should be really within reach of one either at Leicester or Nottm. Will you remember me to your Mother. I like to think of you in that pretty house with her at present.

Yours sincerely, B. M. S. Clough

Miss Clough's letter says —

Dear Miss Dexter,

I hear from my Mother that you are reading Green's History, & she thinks I might perhaps be of use in giving some suggestions as to the best way of reading it. I do not think that at present papers of questions would be of any use to you, but I think you would find it a good plan after you have read carefully one chapter (never a larger division of the book) to make a short — quite short — abstract of what is in it & if you would care to send me the abstracts as you make them, I should be glad to read them over & suggest alterations & make any remarks I could on them.

The great thing to notice in reading & in making abstracts is, not isolated events, but the general tendency & effect in the long run of the series of events during a considerable period of time for instance of the events in the time preceding the Norman Conquest or in the time from the Conquest to the accession of Henry II & so on.

I hope these suggestions may be of some small use to you, & if there is anything I could do in the way of answering questions I should be very glad to hear from you again.

Yours truly, B. A. Clough

Sept 5

Mr N. Richardson (Nottm.) is here today staying with us. He is preaching for us at Crich. I do feel great pleasure in his society. We have been speaking, this morning, over breakfast on various social topics such as the land question — Ireland — the Church etc. I enjoy that kind of conversation more than anything. My brother John is chosen to be organist at Albion Chapel Sneinton, Nottm. We are all very pleased. Miss Kirk & Miss Cowlishaw came for tea yesterday. We had a nice afternoon, music etc. After tea we went a stroll through the quarries then my Father and I went a part of the way home with them. They are very nice girls. Am staying at home from Chapel to help Mother this morning.

Sept 6

Mr R. went home this morning. I accompanied him to the station. We had a delightful sermon last night. Three subjects of meditation he gave viz. "The riches of Christ" in the glory he had with the Father from the beginning, "The poverty of Christ" in taking upon Himself the human form "for our sakes", & "Our future riches" which are vouchsafed unto us because he became poor. "He who was rich yet for our sakes became poor that we through His poverty might be made rich."

Have written to Mr Packer today asking if there be a vacancy under the Nottingham School Board.

Sept 14th

Mr Griffiths has been and gone. Everybody at Crich was extremely satisfied with his discourses both in the morning & afternoon. "A way of escape" Cor 1. X. 13 was his afternoon text, Gal. VI.2 "Bear ye one another's burdens etc." at night. Father, Mother & I went to Mrs Young's at Crich where he stayed, for tea on Sunday. It rained all day more or less. Yesterday morning I walked with father to Ambergate Station. He went to Leicester by the same train as Mr. G. In the afternoon went to the Ladies tea meeting at Crich. It was a relief to go for I felt greatly depressed, with overwhelming thoughts.

Miss Clough wrote yesterday that she considered it best for me to read Green straight through first. I am 21 tomorrow.

Sept 15

My birthday. Received several letters with cards of congratulations from my friends this morning. It is a beautiful day so bright & clear sun shining all day. No party — all quiet — with my dear Father & Mother. I am now a woman. I feel one in point of experience. My girlhood gone! And, yet, I do not look back to it with regret. I mean I don't grieve that I am getting older. Many have been the sad hours that I have spent up to the present and I feel it would be terrible to live them again. Of course I have had joys, but the sorrows are more vividly before me just now. I prayed to the Lord this morning, & gave myself anew in consecration to Him, asking for the Holy Spirit to dwell in me & perfect me in every good word & work. O! that I may be lowly in heart.

As I resume this writing the sun is shedding his dying glory in at my bedroom window. The sky is, as it were, on fire. God grant that so may be the close of my life glorious & beautiful, gladdening to all who behold. The valley looks lovely bathed in soft light. I feel a holy calm, no troubled thoughts now. How gracious God is — giving us these seasons of repose after the fierce conflicts that have shaken our souls; at those times — although the "heavens are as brass", yet if we will only be still and not let our mind be overbalanced there will be a "way of escape" for He will not let us be "tried above that we are able". His leadings are mysterious, but let us only trust & hope & all will eventually be right. God grant it. Humility is what I most need, to be humble in everything. This is on one of the cards which was sent this morning. "He will fulfil the desire of those that fear Him. He also will hear their cry and will save them."

Sept 19 Sunday

A lovely summer day. Father brought me more presents on Friday from Derby which had been sent by John from Nottingham. My dear Brother sent me a box of oil colours, palette, brushes, canvas etc. for he knew I had long wished for them. My Aunt Jane sent Japanese glove & handkerchief boxes and a bottle of scent with a lock of her white hair — she is seventy one years old.

This letter came from her with the presents.

9 Peas Hill Rise
Sept. 15th 1886

My Dear Niece,
   It is your birthday today and a bright sunny one too, and I do sincerely
hope and pray long and many may be in store for you. Clouds may &
will rise, but the blessed sunshine dispels them all. Lo may the Sun of
Righteousness dispel all that may rise in your path, and this He will do if
we only trust Him and ask His help in every time of need. Dear Gracie,
will you please accept this small token of love for your birthday? Two
boxes, one for your handkerchiefs & the other for your gloves. I would
like to have sent them full, but cannot do so now. I am so sorry to hear
your dear Father is so unwell but trust he may soon recover. How is the
spot on his tongue? Should be glad to hear, and about your dear
Mother's arm. Give my best love to them and receive my dear niece the
same with my best wishes for your present and eternal welfare.
   I remain your dear Aunt,
      Jane Dawkins.

I copy this so that in future years should the original letter get lost I may
see the expressions penned by my honoured Aunt. Her life has been spent
for others — always doing — always bearing the burdens of those around
her. On another slip of paper, containing a lock of her hair she says,
   "Dear Gracie, I have sent you a few of my grey hairs & you will not
   despise them on that account for you once asked me for some. Well here
   they are, and it says somewhere, 'Grey hairs are honourable <u>if found in
   the way of righteousness</u>.'
      From your dear Aunt Jane, 71"

I do prize them, immeasurably & shall — when I am able to buy one —
wear them in a gold locket.
   My brother wrote this <u>himself</u> to me:

      "To my sister Grace on her 21st Birthday
   Thou hast a soul by God refined
   Scion of that fair pair which

Sixty centuries ago was placed
In Eden by His hand.
Mystically preserved and cultivated life
Through dark long ages.
Herein with vicissitude of empires raised and fallen.
Sometimes the slender thread of life
Perchance has run thro' veins of noblemen
In climes far distant & in generations old
Then to all human view been lost
In the great sea of life which flows
Around our globe.
These things, the care of great Omniscience to trace,
Thine to use the golden talents by Him bestowed
And let th' implanted sense of grace
Teach thy hand figures ought to trace
And heaven-given taste show how to fill
Thy colours, brilliant or soft, until
The canvas all aglow, with energy replete
Shall preach, to generations after thee
The great conceptions inspired from
His Great Book of Life."

I don't think to realise his conceptions in the last few lines, but I shall try my best to learn how to paint. I shall be delighted to try.
  Yesterday dear Lucie Miers with her sisters Annie & Pattie, came to see me. They have invited me to go with them next Saturday to Liverpool to the Exhibition. How kind! I am going (*DV*[31]). This morning had a communication from the Nottm. School Board to say I am one of the selected candidates next Tuesday to go to Nottm. to appear before the School Management Committee. I am entirely in the Lord's hands. Let Him do what seemeth Him good. Everything will be right, I know in the end. There has been nothing but pleasure for me since after Monday. First one thing then another has come in the shape of letters, cards, presents, invitations, etc. to cheer me. I feel the sweet quiet of trusting altogether in God. I want to live for Him, to think of Him, to love Him supremely. I

---

[31] *Deo Volente* = God Willing

want Him to be my all in all. No worries — no desires — no plans — except those I <u>know</u> to be in harmony with His divine will, for this reason I pray to have all spiritual graces, to be able to conform in all matters to Him. To have no will of my own, but to glorify my God & Saviour. I have found & proved that this only can ensure present & eternal happiness. I know, as my dearest Aunt says, sometimes the clouds will gather — as they have done in the past but the sun will shine all the brighter afterwards, and after the night of sorrow there will be "Eternal Joy". O glorious thoughts. To enjoy the endless happiness of the purified — the redeemed. That state is worth toiling & suffering for. This life after all is but a fleeting dream when compared to the endless existence hereafter.

Sept 26

How shall I write all that I have seen this week. Went to Nottingham on Tuesday in consequence of correspondence with Mr Packer. Am not qualified as an Assistant till I know the result of Scholarship Exam. Stayed in N. till Friday morning — enjoyed it very much.

Friday in Derby — went to Art Gallery, Museum etc. Came home with Father at night. Saturday — Liverpool. Never saw so much in a day before. Went with Mr Miers — at their expense — in a <u>first</u> <u>class</u> <u>saloon</u> carriage. Visited Walker's Art Gallery, the museum, Royal Exchange; saw St George's Hall, went through the Mersey Tunnel, back across the river, inspected the docks, had a very good <u>dinner,</u> then to the Exhibition. O how interesting. People of all nationalities selling their wares of all kinds. Ludiem(?) Village, Music etc. What pleasure to me to see these things. So thankful to Mr Miers for asking me to go. He wants me to go with them to a grand concert at Matlock Bath on Friday. We started at 6 am & got home about 10.30 pm. It is Sunday today. So quiet here — sun shining — after all the excitement of yesterday. What a wonderful place Liverpool is. Poverty & riches all together side by side — in the Royal Exchange we saw men — probably with millions — in the streets there poor little arabs, no shoes or stockings, selling books, toys, matches etc. One poor woman sitting on a doorstep had a shawl on, from under which peeped a baby's tiny hand. That little white hand has been present to me ever since. The poor woman had matches to sell. My heart was filled with pity at these sights. When will things be more equal? Why is it that such wealth and great poverty exist side by side in England? These things ought to be altered.

Sept 30

Finished my first picture in oil colours yesterday. No tuition. My Father & Mother think it is very well for the first attempt. It is a little scene which I conceived as I proceeded to paint.

Had a letter from Mrs Clough on the 28th & also one from a gentleman connected with the High Pavement School Nottm. as follows

High Pavement Day Schools
Nottingham Sep 26th 1886

Dear Madam,

Are you still seeking a situation in Nottingham. We are looking out for an Assistant — Girl's Department — Salary £35 or £40 a year.
Kindly inform me if you think this in your way.

Yours very truly, William Hugh
Miss Dexter, please forward copy of Testimonials .

I shall not go if I find it connected with the Unitarians.[32]

Oct 2nd

Went last evening with Mr & the Misses Miers to a concert at the Pavilion, Matlock Bath. The sole artistes were Madam Norman Neruda & Mr Charles Hallé. I had not been to a concert of that description, for more than two years, so that I the more appreciated it, especially the skill displayed by Madame Neruda on the violin. I was entranced. Drove home with the Miers & family. Stayed all night & returned this morning home. A letter came from the High Pavement School to say they had made a provisional appointment. It is all for the best I am sure.

Oct 10

Received information last week that I was successful at the Admission Exam, and obtained a place in the third class. I am so pleased I have passed though only third class, almost entirely by my own exertions for I had very little help with my studies, having to ponder over & find the solution of any

---

[32] It was actually one of the first non-sectarian schools in the country but situated close to High Pavement (Unitarian) Chapel, "the finest dissenting church in town" (Wright's TD, 1887) which dominated the street.

difficulty that presented itself. Then I missed the two last years of my apprenticeship 3rd & 4th year P. T. exams, which, in addition to the previous two year's work I had to look up, made a good nine or ten months work for me, so taking these things into consideration I feel satisfied in passing this scholarship examination as I have done.

Father & I went to a political meeting at Crich last night — Mr Jacoby M.P. was there & spoke, besides other gentlemen. He has or appears to have sound radical opinions but they gave him to understand that — should his views change, that he would not conscientiously be able to fully represent their views in Parliament, then they would choose another representative. They (his constituents) seem delighted with him at present. It poured with rain when we came from the meeting so that we were very wet when we got home. Poor politicians!

Oct 31

My Father, Mother and I went to London on Oct 14th for one day. It was my Mother's first visit there. We saw the British Museum, with its interesting specimens of Assyrian sculpture (1600 B.C.) and many things at which we were astonished & delighted. In the interior of St Paul's & Westminster Abbey, we saw the monuments & read the inscriptions to England's great men. After seeing these things we went to the Colonial & Indian Exhibition. The skill of the Colonists; with the natural beauty of the products as fruits, timber etc., were, we thought amazing. Although we had not the opportunity owing to scarcity of time, to see nearly all over. It was a very fine day, so that there was nothing which marred our enjoyment. I have had no chance of writing about it before. Painted my second picture — a copy of woman's head.

On 12th November Grace was engaged at St Peter's Schools in Broad Marsh, Nottingham. The school Log Book notes on 26th November that:
"...Stand[ard]s I & II decidedly improving under the new assistant Miss Dexter." **On 4th December 1886 her appointment was made permanent.**[33]

---

[33]   St Peter's Trust Log Book 1874-97 (girls).

◆1887◆

Jan 7

I have been in a situation in Nottingham for about six weeks, I am home now for my Christmas holidays. I am at S. Peter's Schools. Return on Monday the 10th inst. My salary is £40 a year. I am able to support myself entirely. How thankful I feel for this. I want to write a deal more but cannot yet. We have had such a happy Xmas. The first time I have been away from home!

April 3

Nearly 3 months since I wrote anything here! I am always so busy. It is our School exam. on 26th and I am studying for my certificate next Decr. and attending drawing classes at the School of Art. I scarcely ever have a minute to spare. But this (Sunday) afternoon I thought I would write a little in my journal. I am still living with my brother & sister [in law] although I may not be for much longer as they are thinking of leaving the town. I like the teachers at S. Peter's. Miss Aram is very kind and free with us. I teach Standards I & II. I hope they will pass well at the exam. I had another letter from Miss F. Nightingale a month or two ago. This is her letter.

Jan 22nd 1887
10 South St
Park Lane N.

My Dear Grace

I was very glad to hear from you and I hope that I may believe that you are happy at S. Peter's Schools — and that you were very fortunate in getting a post there & so near home.

Tell me about your children & how you manage them and I will tell you that I hope you are not sitting up at night, or ever getting your feet wet or reading too many political speeches — but taking reasonable care to keep your "temple of the Holy Spirit" in good health. We were very glad that you were successful at the "Scholarship Exam.", and I suppose you are now studying for your certificate, wherefore I write these few hints, and should be very glad to know how you are going on. Your account of

Mr Aitkin's Mission interested me very much. May we all remember
such seasons in our practical daily work in God's Name as Christ would
have done it, did do it when he was here even as a Village Workman —
and this is not an effort or constraint but as He did remembering His &
our Father's infinite love, & feeling it as a home to do God Divine
Service every day and not only at Church, thinking of Him in everything
as the "handmaid of the Lord" & doing everything as Christ, the Lover of
our souls "would have it done, making it our Father's business," as He
did, & commending our mind & spirit our whole life into our Father's
hands as He did. This is my prayer for you & I am sure it is yours for
me.

Christ was such a lover of little children like yours. If I have not written
before, you will know that it is because I am so overworked & have little
strength for it. Heartily tho' late in sending are always my New Year's
wishes for you.
Ever Dear Grace
Yours with the deepest interest, F. Nightingale
I send a card of animals for the little children.

She sent me three beautiful cards, one for the children which I am going to
have framed & two for myself. What a dear thoughtful lady she is to
remember me and write when I have done with Lea School. I do feel that I
am highly favoured in receiving my letter from one so illustrious.

I went yesterday to see Sir Noel Paton's great picture "Vigilante et Orate".
It is being exhibited for a short time in Nottingham by special permission of
Her Majesty. A most wonderful picture. The chief part of interest being to
my mind, the expression of Our Lord's countenance. When after the first
time of praying that " if it were possible the cup might pass from Him" He
comes & finds His disciples sleeping and looking at them says the words of
which the picture is a representation. What weight of thought, care, sorrow,
intermingled with compassion, love, patience, shepherdly love are depicted
in that worn, weary, loving face. The eyes reveal as it were, the thoughts &
feelings of Our Blessed Lord & Saviour, as in that hour of deep agony,
when the mastery over sin and death had to be gained, he bore the sins of the
world, and was left alone to "tread the wine-press". O, should not the
contemplation of the Son of God in His humility all absorbing love for

1 Burton St (now Burnham St), Sherwood (white-fronted house on L.) Grace's family were living here in 1884.

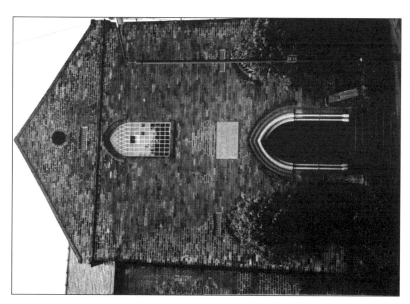

The National School, Penn Lane, Melbourne. John Dexter was teaching here in 1851.

"Cousin Sarah"

Sarah Young Weigel

Aunt Jane Dawkins, aged 99

Sneinton Board School, Notintone St. Grace's first teaching appointment c. 1879
Photo: Jim Freebury, 1968

John Dexter in old age
painted by his grandson
Giovanni Hermon

Badly damaged photo of
Beaty as a young woman

Group at Aunt Jane's
100th birthday, 1915:

Grace is in centre of
back row, husband
Herbert Dupree is
extreme left of photo,
and Cousin Mary
Dawkins (in white
boa) is bottom right.

DEPARTMENT OF SCIENCE AND ART OF THE COMMITTEE OF
HER MAJESTY'S MOST HONOURABLE PRIVY COUNCIL
ON EDUCATION.

AT the SECOND GRADE Examination in Model
Drawing, held on the 28th April, 1892,
28,794 candidates presented themselves. The results
were :—

1st Class	... ...	3,728
2nd Class	...	8,369
Failed	...	16,697

This is to certify that

Grace J. Dexter

aged _26_, obtained a First Class in
the above-named Subject.

By order,

[signature]

mankind constrain us to offer ourselves a "living sacrifice to God which is our reasonable service." With these thoughts I must waive inscribing more.

I go home on Thursday next for a few days. It is Easter. I shall soon see my dear Mother & Father!

May 19

Just a minute to spare before going to my certificate class. My Brother John & family have gone to live at Belper & I am in lodgings at Mrs Brown's. Our school exam is over, my two classes Stands. I & II passed 84 p.c. each. I thought they would have done better, but I must content myself with the knowledge that I did my best in preparing them for it, only having them five months. I have no teacher to help me yet with the two classes. It is very hard work — between 60 & 70 children every day, but I feel so thankful that I have such good health. I scarcely know what it is to be idle a minute. To think that I am in lodgings! Well, I wonder what the next event in my career will be. John came last week for a few days on business & he came again last night. I am so glad to see him now. Anyone from home is so welcome. My dear, dear Mother came a week or two ago, only for a day but wasn't it delightful to me! Home again next week — Whitsuntide — Jubilee Year — holidays in June again — O, what fine prospects. Everything has the word Jubilee prefixed to it. We are expecting grand rejoicings in the country this 50th year of Her Majesty's reign. I should like to go to London on 21st June — I wonder if I shall. Well I must go to my class now it is high time I started. I wish I had more time to write here in this book. I forget everything I want to say when I am in such a hurry.

May 25

Went tonight to hear the Blue Hungarian Band by myself. The music was charming. So skilfully & sweetly executed. On Monday we had a "grand miscellaneous concert" at school. A great success. Room crowded. Many could not obtain entrance owing to crush. — Children looked very nice & performed their parts very well indeed. I played two accompaniments that was all. Two or three good short speeches from the Managers & schoolmaster. I felt so happy amongst the dear children which happiness lasted all night & next day. Then came a bit of depression & now I feel happy again after this music. Ah, how circumstance influences me. Well, I shall soon be at home. Two more days & then, happy thought!

June 3

Have been at home a week. Monday went to see John at Belper. Tuesday
& Wednesday was confined indoors with neuralgia — yesterday, Thursday
went with my dear Mother to Rowsley, thence to Chatsworth & Haddon.
What a contrast the two places present. Chatsworth in all its modern
magnificence with its lofty, splendidly furnished rooms, and its great
conservatory covered by 70,000 sq. ft. of glass, and heated by 7 miles of hot
water piping — to Haddon with all its grandeur "faded & gone". Its empty
apartments — save one or two in which a remaining bed or chairs or an old
dining table arrested the interest — spoke to one of decay and the passing
away of all terrestrial things. I was considerably more interested in the latter
than the former place as is invariably the case with me. When new or old
are in question the ancient has a fascination to my mind, to which modern
things are as having no power. To recall scenes that had been transacted
there in that old hall in imagination, to live more than two or three hundred
years ago, and see that stately home filled at the feast and banquet with the
high spirited, full of life and vigour, of courage, and hope. To see them
sitting at the board and to hear the laugh and jest, and then the cup which
when filled was to be emptied, or the penalty, for not drinking the supposed
necessary portion, to be to the certain discomfiture of the unfortunate guest,
the reception of the remaining contents by the sleeve of his coat which was,
for the purpose placed in a hand-fetter until the operation was completed.
Then to witness the gay ball-room with its carved cornice and crested
ornamentations, all alive with the voices and movements in the merry dance,
and faces, speaking of hope and desire in life. But I am going on too far. I
must stop. I was thinking of Dorothy Vernon & her flight on the night of her
sister's marriage festival. We saw the steps by which she escaped. O, I
could have lingered hours thinking of them all! But — Ah, there are not
many rhapsodical beings like me I think. I seldom find any. Most people
like the things of today in preference to those of yore. Perhaps after all it is
better to live more in the present. Well, I shall do so next week — on
Monday I return to school where all my dreaming will end for a while.

July 1

On June 21st I went with my brother to London — it being Jubilee day —
and we saw all the great sight of the Royal Procession. To see them go to
the Westminster Abbey we stood in Regent St. but had not so good a view

as we had on their return, when we stationed ourselves in Cockspur St. From our position there (on the edge of the causeway) we were enabled to see her Majesty and all the Royal Princes and Princesses, and the foreign kings and queens with the Indian Princes, who were mounted and looked very picturesque in their native dress. It was a very grand pageant, the likes of which I had never seen (of course!)

The queen was smiling, when she passed by us, and I thought she looked a great deal nicer than her photographs represent her to look. Then the illuminations were beautiful. Almost every house, besides the great shops and other business places, at the West End were illuminated in some way either more or less elaborate. We walked about — with the surging crowd that thronged the streets — till 11 o'clock when we took the 'bus to King's Cross. In the morning of the same day we started from Nottm. @ 11.15 a.m. and did not get back till 5 o'clock the next morning. My feet were so painful and swollen for a day or two after. It did not seem to affect John at all. But he is used to walking, I suppose that was the reason.

I am very glad I went. My brother and I spent such a pleasant day in each other's company moralising and philosophising on all that we saw and heard. We always suit each other when together. O, how I should like to live in London. I have always said so since I first went — now I have been there three times, and more than ever I feel it would be so delightful to live in that great city. The buildings are magnificent.

The following passage illustrates some of the difficulties facing teachers: not only did they have to teach large classes all day, they were then expected to go round collecting school fees in the evenings! Teachers were employed to get results, whatever the circumstances, and Miss Aram, the Mistress under whom Grace worked, was forced to resign because the percentages were not adequate in the examination.

Well, I must stop in writing of London. Now for domestic or rather school affairs. Dear Miss Aram left us yesterday. I am so sorry on her account and on ours as well, but: this question of percentages is the cause. Because we didn't get so high a one — not withstanding great disadvantages — which the Managers thought ought to have been the case, the headmistress must be asked to resign, and thus make way for one whom they think <u>will</u> get the results. I am sure we are like machines and the poor children get no easy time of it; for we are obliged to harass and threaten in order to get a high rate p.c. at the Examinations. Miss Dale and I are going to Miss Aram's tomorrow (Sat.) to see her and take her a little present. We are losing such a kind, sympathetic friend. Our new Mistress comes on Monday. O, I do wish we had free education![34] I have had to deal with such heart-rending cases of poverty this week — in getting or trying to get arrears for school money. Actually one poor woman had to borrow the money, they had not a farthing belonging to themselves. Just a few shillings a week — and often not that — to maintain a family upon. The trade is terribly bad here and elsewhere. When will things mend. I felt deeply grieved at hearing these accounts of the misery existing in homes in England, so it is, but surely it should not be so! Where is the legislation that permits such a state of things. People not knowing where to get a mouthful of bread — independent of charity — in this rich and fertile land of ours. And if these poor people apply to the Guardians to remit their school fees they get shamefully insulted, by impertinent questions, and so forth, till they tell me they would almost rather starve or do anything than apply for relief. I cannot write more now but these are dreadful facts.

July 8

Our new headmistress came on Monday. Her manner with the children is much to be admired. She has such a cheerful yet authoritative way of dealing with them. Exceedingly systematic as she has proved so far, and will expect us to be, yet I think we shall like her. It does not do to conclude that we shall be dissatisfied with people before we know what they are. But still we miss dear Miss Aram's kind, free, and sympathetic presence & conversation. There has been a change in the organisation already. My pupil teacher has been taken in to the large room & I have now to manage Stands. I & II by myself without any help except half an hour or so in the morning. It will be <u>very</u> hard work, for there are 87 children on the registers. I hope my strength will be equal to the task, then I don't mind at all. I feel very, very tired after my day's work. I am now going to Mr Brown's (my certificate class) for three hours from 6.30 to 9.30 p.m. So the days go by. Each one with its ever returning routine. But the Lord upholds us and fortifies us for all our duties, therefore to Him be the Praise forever.

---

[34]   June 12 1891 Sir William Hart Dyke, MP, introduced a bill to abolish school fees in elementary schools. It was passed August 1891.

Sometimes — when very weary — I grow rather desponding, but always endeavour to check myself on the recollection of all my mercies. "Not more than others I deserve, Yet God has given me more." O, that not a murmuring thought might ever possess my mind, or a dissatisfied word escape my lips, but that my heart might always be overflowing with thankfulness to our Gracious Father, who so richly blesses, and endues us with His grace.

I had a sweet letter from my dearest Mother on Tuesday and one yesterday from dear Annie Miers. These are pleasing helps on the way of life. Human sympathy, ah! What is not comprehended in that expression. All — to some natures that constitutes either happiness or misery, lightheartedness, or oppressive sorrow. To feel that other kindred hearts, beat in unison with your own, that theirs rejoice when you rejoice, and weep when yours is overwhelmed with grief. This is indeed a thing because of which we may rejoice and be grateful. This divinely implanted feeling is worthy of cultivation and should be, by all means, prized, both by those in whose possession it lies, and also by those unto whom its influence is extended.

July 18

Went last night (Sunday) to Stoney St. Chapel to hear Mr Lacey, a young student at the Baptist college, who is going to India as a missionary. He spoke very beautifully to young people from the parable of the Prodigal Son, and besought his young hearers to keep steadfastly by their Heavenly Father's side and not by the foolish desire for so-called independence to wander into paths which will but terminate in ruin and remorse. It was the last time he would have the opportunity of preaching in that chapel for perhaps many years, and consequently his pleadings were all the more earnest and eloquent. My cousin Mary[35] and I stayed to the prayer meeting at the close of the former service, and what with the thoughts of other years, and friends with whom I had commingled my prayers and songs in that vestry, and who were no longer there — together with the emotions I felt at the thought of the young preacher going to a foreign land to sow the seed on soil perhaps on which no other hand had ever bestowed care, and also the prayers on his behalf which were offered full of Christian love and sympathy, these combined to overwhelm me with mingled feelings of joy and

---

[35]   Aunt Jane's daughter, Mary Dawkins, b. 1844.

sadness; joy, for the noble self-sacrifice occasioned by the constraining love
of Christ, for the beauty of the religion that engendered and evoked such
self-sacrifice, for the blessing of Christian friends whose hearts beat in
unison, and whose aims and hopes are one; sorrow, for sin, for the evil of
my own heart, for energies wasted, duties undischarged, principles
sacrificed. The tears poured down my cheeks. I could not restrain them. I
thought of the days when every Sunday evening I had sat side by side with
my dear Mother, and when my Father offered up many a prayer there, of
dear Maria who had many times joined in worship with us there, and left us
for the glory of Heaven. Of the dear Christian brethren and sisters who had
from time to time gathered in prayer around that room. Of the ministers
who from time to time sat at the table and who had passed away, some to
their heavenly home, and others to distant scenes. With these images
crowding upon my mind, is it to be wondered at that I was overcome? I
shook hands with Mr Lacey and wished him — with all my heart — God
speed. He was very grateful for the kind expressions of the friends to him,
for his welfare and success in his — I must say — <u>glorious</u> undertaking. He
asked us to pray for him and I am sure we shall. At least I will, fervently,
for I can conceive of no higher calling than that of a bearer of the precious
Gospel of Christ to a benighted world. When outside the chapel Mr Stent,
the organist, asked my cousin and me to join the choir. I was very pleased,
for I have wished to settle somewhere a long time. So I shall, if the Lord
wills, go when I come back from my Midsummer holidays. Next week I go
<u>home</u>!

Aug 31
Have been back at school nearly three weeks. Spent a very desirable
vacation at home during which time — what with going out, receiving
friends and private study — I had no opportunity or rather did not make any
— to write in this journal.
   Our new school mistress is very exacting in school work, we have to work
so hard. This week I have neuralgia very bad again — never had it before
since my coming to Nottm. I think it is with harassment that has brought it
on. Well, I must bear it till the time comes for me to have things go a little
easier with me. Have sat in the choir at S.S. two Sundays — feel more
settled in that respect now. It only wants about three months to our
certificate exam! Oh, how I hope I shall pass.

Sept 2

The teachers at S. Peter's all went by invitation to the Rectory[36] to an "at home". We passed a very pleasant time from five to half past seven. Singing and conversation were the order of the evening. Admiral Sullivan, Mrs Edgcome's brother was very entertaining. He sang, "I fear no foe in shining armour." Subsequently he brought in a large book with plates illustrative of the Crimean War. Seating himself next to me with the book on a gypsy table, he vividly explained all that then transpired, describing — from the pictures — the position of the contending forces and frequently showing the ship in which he himself was for the time stationed, interspersing his narrative when alluding to himself by interesting and sometimes amusing incidents which then took place. I was so deeply interested in this narrator — who had actually taken active part in the engagements he was describing — that, seeing how attentive I was, he addressed nearly all his remarks to me, though several others were listening. This makes twice that events relating to the Crimea have been rehearsed to me by distinguished eye witnesses — Miss Nightingale and Admiral Sullivan. I cannot but think I am greatly favoured by this apparent coincidence in the case of one as humble in station. Oh, it was nice to be there. I often think to associate with people of that class must be highly gratifying. But this is not the end of our existence. There will be a hereafter state when — to the extent of our desires — we shall mingle with the great and good that have been in all ages — our highest powers will there be developed and we shall have communion with congenial spirits for ever.

Sept 14

The eve of my twenty-second birthday. I have no leisure time now and yet I am stealing a little tonight to write in here. Twenty-two! how old I am getting. I remember the time when I thought I should never be twenty-one, and now another year past — even that has gone. And what is there to show for it? Very little outwardly — or to be clearer — I don't know what particular good I have done to anybody. Daily toil has been my portion so far, but I fear it has been often with murmuring thoughts on my lot in life — that I have performed my duties. On the other hand, inwardly I feel I have advanced. My spirit more subdued, and I can take all events calmly,

---

36   The Rector of St Peter's Church was Revd. George Edgcombe, 1870-1906.

trusting in Him who has said, "I will never leave thee, nor forsake thee." The evenness of my life and feelings has never been disturbed by anything during the last year or so; and yet, I long for a closer walk with God. As the years still pass by, I hope to keep progressing in beauty of life and character and then, with new ideas as to the object of life — namely that of progression in all ways — instead of bringing regret for the loss of youthful days these birthdays will be but welcome landmarks in the course of time, indicating our nearness to the goal of His which it is our endeavour to reach. May God grant that another anniversary of this kind may find me purer in heart and more fitted for His Kingdom than at present.

Sept 17
My birthday is gone once more. It has been such a happy time though — so many dear friends have remembered me with good wishes and presents. My dear Father and Mother sent me letters which gave me more joy than I can tell. They say how great a blessing I am to them, and that the favour of the Lord was shown in giving me at a time when they were losing other dear children and their hearts were sad. They have always spoken of me as the comforter sent in their time of trouble, and my dear Father says my name — Grace Jane — "is very, very dear to us, recalling memories of the past now most happily realised beyond our thought or expectation, for when Herman & Priscilla Jane & Hepzibah Milton were taken above we wanted a mark of favour and consolation from heaven and it was given us in yourself and so our Grace was rightly named and still proves a Grace and Glory to our growing old age and whether you were named after your dear Aunt who first received you into her arms, or after your dear grandmother of most precious memory to me, in either case you may feel it an honour to be called after them." Further he continues — "Well my dear, dear child it is something indeed for you to feel and enjoy that you are all to us that a parent can wish — equipped by the Thrice blessed Bestower with favour as a robe in sight of God and Man, and for which we often and always give God the thanks — Pursue, my dear child the destiny marked out for you without doubt or fear conscious of His divine leading & he will give you yet more grace, for His bounties & gifts — who shall limit, to those whom He loves?" He closes— "A Dieu. Au Revoir my beloved daughter, keep growing in the knowledge of our most dear Lord Jesus, nor will you be without the manifestation of His loving Presence."

Surely these words from my beloved Father, together with those of my Mother — "May the Lord cause his face to shine upon you and give you health and strength and every other blessing both spiritual & temporal out of the fullness of His great treasury," surely these words, I say, ought to inspire me with fresh courage for the future battles in life. Strong in faith, and equipped with the whole armour of God. What shall come amiss to us?

Tomorrow is the last Sunday [Sept 18th 1887] at dear old Stoney St. Chapel. It is to be closed as a place of worship after then. Mr Griffiths is coming to preach the last sermons.

❧1888❧

A gap of eight months ensues before Grace's next entry. The family are still at Whatstandwell but not in good shape; Grace is unemployed, her father has been ill and by September they have taken in two lodgers to make ends meet.

May 30th

O, what a long time since last I wrote here — now I have only a minute or two to spare but the desire took possession of me to write a word or two just now. I have been at home since last November[37] — took my certificate in December — but have not yet gained another situation. My dear Father has been ill over a month with bronchitis and cannot yet go out. Mary is at home too. This has been a hard time for us but with dear Father's recovery we trust things will turn. I was at Leicester, staying with my cousins for about a month just after Easter. I had a very nice time of it. They have written to say I can go & be there till I hear of something, if I like. How kind of them. But I feel so thankful to have been at home just now for I have been able to wait upon my beloved Father & Mother. They are glad too that I have been with them. I have tried after several situations but have failed to gain an appointment. There are so many teachers seeking work. I really think, should nothing open out here, of going to one of the Colonies, for I do so long to be of help to my Mother & Father. They have done so much for me. I am trying to wait patiently and trust in the Lord my Strength. The afflictions do indeed develop in us greater spiritual life &

---

37   According to the Log Book she left St. Peter's Schools on Friday 18th November 1887.

51

earnestness of purpose. I feel and know that this illness of Father's has drawn me closer to Him by the outpouring of my soul in supplication for his recovery and that we may serve Him better with renewed health & strength. Every day I long for a closer walk with God.

Sept 15

I am 23 today. Still at home. Very busy just now having two living with us who work at the saw-mill. I am very glad it is so as I am at home, between us Mother and I are just earning a little. Am waiting an opportunity of beginning a school of my own — should prefer it to again engaging in a public school — meantime as far as possible am practising music, French etc. Twenty three! Oh that is getting on — soon thirty now. I prayed this morning very earnestly that this year might be better spent than all past years. Life is drifting away & what am I doing while? This thought often presses me, what account shall I give if all these years allotted time for improvement, & in which to do good. God grant that I may use and improve all my time.

We have had a friend, Miss Richardson from Manchester staying with us a fortnight. She returned home last night — we have been delighted with her company — so lively, pleasant & withal good. I have much enjoyed the walks we have had with her in these beautiful country lanes. "Society, friendship & love are indeed Divinely bestowed upon man." What should we do without these refreshing, helpful times of intercourse with friends whom we love & respect. Continually striving to live in thought, word & deed — aright — ever active in mind thereby having no chance retrogression — the object in view being that of living for others — excluding every selfish feeling & motive — this must be the ideal life — how hard to attain! Indeed it seems at times an agony to crucify self and to pursue a course of noble "self annihilation" of which Carlyle speaks. Many a time I get weary of brain and almost despondent. When, in my own small way, I realise the magnitude of the purpose of life — and what to my idea a perfect being should be. My head aches now with thinking therefore I must rest from writing. O for strength oftener to think and embody in practical demonstration grand, glorious heaven born thoughts which sometimes are conceived after patient unremitting search for truth — prayerful appeals for wisdom — difficulties bravely faced & conquered. As I write the glorious sun has just burst upon me from behind a dark cloud. What an emblem of our Father who shines with glorious beams of love when all around us seems dark & full of sadness. God grant that this day may be the beginning of a glorious era in my life.

❧1889❧

Feb 15th

On reading over the above — written on my birthday I find myself still to continue in the same strain of thought. Life full of purpose — activity — zeal in the course of right in whatever form. But these are only <u>thoughts.</u> I <u>do</u> very little. Activity outside my own domestic sphere is a rare thing with me. Still I am trusting that this time of gathering knowledge scanty though it may be — may find opportunity in due time to disseminate itself for good. O I do so want to benefit those around me though my exertions may be ever so humble. To use our minds in perfectible deep thought should be an immense pleasure to us, and yet how often by the strain we are wearied and turn to think of trifles requiring no lofty height of comprehension. How glorious if our poor, weak beings could realise it and retain the same would be the state of constant elevated conception, but alas! that must remain for some of us at least, till the restored powers in a future world shall confer the boon.

We are in rather low water as far as worldly circumstances are concerned — just now my Father having left the saw-mill and joined my brother in the timber travelling. It may be better soon, meantime I regret that I cannot be earning anything. We may leave here before long — then I hope to begin a school. To be at home as a help to dear Mother in the house, and yet to be doing something to maintain myself is what I should desire.

How difficult it is to find out what is right. Wrong and right seem to me so often commingled that I have to bring all the distinguishing power of which I am possessed to assist in their separation. There must be a truly right way in everything and yet that which is wrong oftime looks so plausible that we follow it as right — this must be though when we do not weigh things over so carefully or look as deep as we might for the principle which <u>right</u> demands. I have thought lately what a grand quality is discretion, how ennobling to those who use it ever with wisdom. What a happy world this would be if this discretion became an underlying power of all action. We do things often so thoughtlessly or are propelled by passion or biased by infatuation for selfish motives (or equally unworthy) — that calm, discreet judgement and action is a rare spectacle.

27th May: *The Alfreton & Belper Journal* **reported that the Robin Hood sawmill had been almost completely destroyed by fire the previous week. That Grace does not mention it, seems to indicate that they had already moved to Belper, her father having changed jobs again.**

In the same issue, she is mentioned as singing "I know that my Redeemer liveth" at the Baptist Sunday School Anniversary in Belper. Grace, her brother John and her father were all musical and are frequently mentioned as performing in church entertainments. Also, in September, Grace took part in a "glee party on behalf of Pleasant Sunday Evenings".[38]

Oct 30

I am spending a week in Manchester with my friends — Richardson[39]. What a great city this is with its teeming throngs wherever you go. The Free Trade Hall is a magnificent place — the carved roof gave me much pleasure — we heard a concert there on Saturday. Sunday we heard the Bishop of M. preach or rather deliver one of a series of lectures on "Christ & His surroundings." "The Unseen World" was the subject of Sunday's lecture, and proved a masterly exposition of the Bishop's view — as concurring to a great extent with those of the scientific men of the day. I enjoyed the service exceedingly. Monday we looked over the Central High Grade Bd. School for boys & girls who have passed the 5th Standard in a previous school. I was much interested in the work going on in schools — and in the appliances for chemistry & cookery & drill etc. which we saw. Monday went with "Cousin" William Richardson to see the Battle of Trafalgar which is a gigantic picture in circular form. You appeared to be standing on the Victory surrounded by the battle ships of French & English. While before you, the central figure, lies Nelson — the great Commander just having received his death wound. We thought it altogether a wonderful representation. The painting being exceedingly realistic. Yesterday a great treat was enjoyed by us for it being the anniversary of the Central Hall

---

[38]   *Alfreton & Belper Journal* 6th Sept. 1889.
[39]   This family appear to have been relatives of the Leicester Richardsons.

Mission — we had the pleasure of hearing the Revs. Hugh Price Hughes & Peter Thompson and other great speakers. O how glorious is the rescue work they are doing in the E. of London. It made one long to be helping them. I told Mr Thompson — on shaking hands with him — that his words had inspired me. I feel that I will go back to my work at Belper determined to do all I can for our Pleasant Sunday Evening Mission[40] — visiting, tract distributing — anything to help this same class of people — but whom <u>Jesus loves</u>. May He help & strengthen me in my resolve.

Nov 1

Yesterday visited the Town Hall. Were shown all the principal apartments therein. It is indeed a magnificent place, the carving and decoration being especially fine. Am staying till Sunday night.

Sunday: Last night went to see one of Mr De Jong's concerts at the Free Trade hall. It was very good. Today heard Dr MacLaren and Mrs Kearney.

New Year's Eve Dec 31st

We have just returned from a meeting held at the Public Hall — our quarterly tea for the people — P.S.E. Mission. We have had a good time —place crowded — first rate entertainment chiefly by boys and girls from Milford School. They have been admirably trained to the reciting of dialogues etc. with which they have delighted us. We — all our family except Mother — are on the committee. Mary & I go round with tracts to visit the people — our object being in this Mission to gather in the poorest & those who have no <u>spiritual home</u> — to our Sunday Night Service where we have, for the present, dioramic views, singing etc. We always have several hundred people there. Mr John Smedley is the prime mover — he is indefatigable, kind and he has the welfare of the people sincerely at heart. I feel glad I am in the work, and must never be weary in well doing — God helping me. Now Mother & Father are gone to bed and I thought I would just take up my pen and write here on the eve of a New Year.

Changes have taken place with us this year. We have left Whatstandwell, that dear, lovely spot, where so many happy days and four years were spent. But we must keep advancing without repining and looking back to the days that are gone. (The bells of S. Peter's are just chiming out 11.30). Well, I

---

40   "Pleasant Sunday Evenings" (or Afternoons), were non-denominational gatherings for poor people; a sort of "home mission".

have been in three schools under the Board here — am now at Cow Hill.
Have had difficulties but will not enter into them now. But dear Father &
Mother are still spared to us — what a blessing! and we have comforts —
food, clothing, shelter, and all these have attended us through the year for
which at its close we would review with thankfulness. John is starting with
a fresh firm tomorrow — "Smithson & Co" of Hull. Father stays with
Newsum's. They sent us a fine turkey which we enjoyed all together on
Christmas Day. Dear Aunt Jane is still alive — we have had no deaths in
the family this year — not of our own relations. How very quickly this year
has gone for me. It seems but the other day since last New Year's Eve. So
life ebbs away and we as it were perceive it not! O how I want my life to be
fruit-bearing, full of good thoughts, to do something always to make lives
better, to raise, comfort, strengthen, bless, wherever I go. I do trust that this
year may find me more advanced than ever I have been in all that is good
and noble. I don't strive and watch enough and evil seems easier than good,
therefore it wants repelling constantly. We begin school again on Monday
after a fortnight's holiday. I pray that I may lead & train those dear children
so as to please Our heavenly Father whose they are, and whom I serve and
to whom I must render account. They are very rough children up there, but
they are His — I try to keep that ever before me. The bells are just tolling
the old year out — a dull, muffled, one bell sound.) How I have prayed the
Lord to be with me ever throughout this year — are the bells ringing the
days? I think so. Now they are ringing brightly — the New Year is born!
May gladness fill our hearts and joy and peace abide with us. They are
clashing now joyous and bright full of hope they sound. Now I must go to
bed.

1890

May 24th
It is nearly one o'clock a.m. and I am writing sitting up in bed, in this book.
Have had the tooth-ache all day at school and cannot sleep for it tonight, so
thought I would improve time otherwise spent in <u>moaning</u> by writing. We
have left school today for the Whitsuntide recess for a week. I went to
Nottm. for a few days at Easter but am staying at home this holiday. My

life has been one even routine on the whole since my last entry. It is very uphill work at school for many in my class are, or were, so backward — but I am doing my utmost with them, and trust they will do pretty well at the examination in September. I have been asking God tonight to help me always more and more to set before them a strong, Christlike example. Some of them are dear little things, and the froward <u>must</u> have my especial care if I am possessed of my Master's spirit. I have just finished reading the life of John Howard[41]. What a man! Unceasing labour, when he had found his vocation. His death is very touching at Cherson in Russian Tartary. When on his last journey of love and helpfulness to the oppressed and suffering, truly a glorious career was his. I have read several books lately which have impressed me in various ways. I may say that they are books of which I had heard people speak. Some in terms of commendation, others in those of censure — and wishing to judge for myself I have availed myself of the opportunity afforded by the Belper Subscription Library of which we are members. "Shirley" (by Currer Bell) was the first, then followed "Vanity Fair" (Thackeray), "Jane Eyre" (Brontë), "Robert Elsmere" (Ward). This last has been exercising the mind of many eminent men and has proved a source of much doubt and controversy by its attempt to prove the impossibility of miracles, and its advocacy of other Unitarian principles (for such I took them to be).[42] But the resurrection of Our Lord cannot thus be denied — as being against all natural law — for with God "all things are possible" and the proofs are yet too strong for the believing mind to reject them. May Our Saviour by the power of His risen height keep us from ignoring those vital realities concerning Him.

I keep trying to improve myself in mind and character but so slowly do I seem to make any advance. I like to read books that afford food for reflection and thought but I so often find my mind inactive and wish I could be always thinking good, true, wise thoughts, and then to act upon them. That is the thing — how often we resolve to act upon our ideal thoughts and then come oh, how far short! Never mind, press on, poor soul amid buffets, falls and failures, be immured and strengthened by the difficulties and experiences of the way.

---

[41]   John Howard, prison reformer, 1726-90.

[42]   *Robert Elesmere* by Mrs Humphrey Ward (1888), was a best-seller about a young clergyman who loses his faith and goes to do social work in the East End of London.

Our President of the People's Sunday Mission, Mr John Smedley, has just
returned from a ten weeks tour in the Holy Land, Egypt etc. He is
continually interesting and instructing us by his accounts and descriptions of
customs, scenery etc. He began a discourse last Sunday night on his visit to
the Holy Sepulchre at Jerusalem, and vividly told of the strange worship
mixed with such hatred to one another of the sects gathered together at the
supposed tomb of Him Who came to bring peace & goodwill to men. O, for
true Christianity & brotherly kindness. Our Committee is being
re-organised — we have started a Dorcas Meeting and a Sunday School is
talked of. I want to do all I can for the Mission. We get the people who
attend no place of worship and it is a privilege to help and do them some
good, by the blessing of God.

July 14, Leicester
Am spending the remaining fortnight of my Midsummer holidays here, the
rest, pleasure & company are very acceptable. It seems nice to have money
to enjoy the good things of this life, but my Cousin says, there is
compensation in being poor, even for with increased wealth comes greater
need of wisdom & discretion to use aught, and not be engrossed entirely
with the surroundings attended on riches. We are going this afternoon to
play lawn tennis at Mrs Harvey's.

Aug 6th
I meant to have written more in my journal while at L[eicester] but
neglected from one cause or other so doing. I had a very nice time of it
though — out every day — my cousins are always exceedingly kind —
seem as if they could not tax themselves enough to desire means of
enjoyment for one.
There is one person whose acquaintance I was pleased to renew — Mr E.
Leaverley. He is going to Australia for his health's sake — consumption is
feared — but I trust it will prove to be otherwise. I may have occasion to
mention him again as I hear respecting his health from my cousins. That is
why I write of him now. His affiancée — Miss Hemlington — whom I also
saw is I believe a very nice young lady. I trust they will like to be happy
together. It does me good to go about amongst one's friends as my brother
says, "it enlarges one's ideas." Dear old John! He is always coming out with
some wise saying or other. Now it is hard work at school till the exam next

month. I do hope my class will do well. I have read, while at L. "The Greatest Thing in the World" by Professor Drummond. A book on <u>love</u>. It did me much good. I must read it again.

Sep 6th

Yesterday we had Mr Needham of London and Rev F. Knowles in for tea. My sister Mary is keeping house for Mr. N. She has been there about two months. I believe it will prove a good place for her. She has two maids to help, so only has to superintend. Mr N. appears very agreeable. We all went out in the evening a nice walk round over the meadow and back by the Chevin. He has asked me to go and see them at Xmas so it is a delightful prospect — another visit to London — I am to go for a week. How things work round. I have many times so longed for someone I know to live there, so that I might occasionally go to the City, which ever since my first visit, impressed me so much with its magnitude and greatness in every respect. And now to spend a whole week there. The thought of going causes me as much pleasure almost as it did five years ago when I went to see Miss Nightingale. But I am not quite so enthusiastic at twenty-five as I was at twenty. The wear and tear of everyday life & work tends greatly to induce a settled state of feeling not so much influenced and excited by transpiring events. What a change ten years makes to one! How hope being deferred becomes less buoyant and we come to take things just as we find them without expecting more than we have reasonable grounds for being sure of.

We are still working up for the exam. It is on the 25th inst. What keen competition there is in everything nowadays. If one falls behind in any way another, better qualified, in some respects at least, stands ready to take the place. One must be up to the mark or "Away with you." So the only practical way if we would live and move "creditably" among our fellows, is to "keep up". "Keep up" in the race — but it sometimes taxes us so much that wearied in mind and body we long for rest. And yet a "full life" is a grand life — full of work. But it is an anxious thought — for one's bread — that causes the weariness, and longing for liberty to work according to the bent of one's disposition. But I fear I am writing in a murmuring strain, and I must not, for though I have much that seems hard to me to contend against, yet I have very many blessings — as Mr Knowles said last Sunday morning, "If we weigh in one scale our own misfortunes & hardships (as we

call them) and in the other God's mercies & blessings — with the greatest
gift of all — Himself — which will outbalance?"

Sep 16

Yesterday was my birthday. Twenty-five, only think of it! I left school at
four and went by train to Cromford, thence to Wirksworth. It was a grand
walk — a real hot bright September day. It was the General Baptist District
Conference. Mother & Father drove in the morning with some G. B. friends
from Belper. I met several whom I knew from Derby, Nottm. etc. and
enjoyed myself thoroughly. We saw in a Weslyan Chapel a table erected to
the memory of "Dinah Bede", that noble woman in George Eliott's book. It
was most interesting to me. I have much to be thankful for in having the
opportunity of such pleasant breaks in the daily routine. Now I must go out,
or I would write more.

London, Christmas

Am spending my holidays with my sister. She has a very nice place here.
It is such a treat for me to be in the Great City again, seeing places for
which I have always cherished so deep an interest. I came on Xmas Eve
(Wednesday). Now it is Saturday. We have not been about much yet.
Yesterday I saw Greenwich College etc. What a magnificent hall frescoed
by Sir James Thornhill. It over-awes me to see the magnitude and skill of
men's genius in such places. The paintings representing England's Great
Admirals and Naval Heroes gave me such pleasure. We also saw Nelson's
coats which he wore in the battle of the Nile and in his last engagement on
the "Victory". The moths had made inroads into one of the coats — it
reminded one of the passage, "Where neither moth nor rust doth corrupt"
and we trust he who was the great & valiant wearer of them is there.

Saturday went to S. Paul's. Sunday morning to hear Archdeacon Farrar at
S. Margaret's Westminster and at night to the City Temple, preacher Rev
Arthur Murrell. Both services were a rare treat to me. Today, Monday,
have been to the National Gallery. That also gave me keen enjoyment —
dined in the Strand. Made a few purchases of toys for the children and
returned by tram to New Cross. Now I must write to Belper.

Tuesday went alone to Westminster Abbey, saw every part (which I had
not previously done) wandered about from one tomb or statue to another,
thinking always thinking. Then I took a bus from Trafalgar Sqr to South

Kensington and spent several hours in the Museum. The plaster casts of ideal sculpture taken from the best specimens in Europe filled me again with wonder at such achievements in the skilful use of the chisel — especially Michael Angelo's figures, of Moses and David — how every vein is brought out — and the marvellous work in the pulpit of Pisa. Indeed I was struck with the fact how well, perfectly — with their whole soul engrossed to produce life like models — these men must have wrought. I was delighted to be again in the city — the busy ceaseless rush of life fills me with wonderment.

Wednesday, New Year's Eve

Today we have been to the Crystal Palace. It is a grand place with its various courts and statuary. There were several entertainments going on which we witnessed successively. Mr Charles Godfrey with his band played some good music. Altogether it has been a day I shall not soon forget. This is the first New Year's Eve I have spent away from home — how different to last year! I wonder what this year will bring forth for us. What changes or otherwise will take place — it is unknown but we will trust that our lives may be better and that we may do more good than in the year to which we are just bidding farewell. May God help us to do the right never minding the consequences. We are just off to a watch-night service.

1891

Ist Jan, Thursday

Heavy fog but took a turn in the city — heard General Booth on his "In Darkest England" scheme at the City Temple after which walked on to the British Museum, where I spent several hours examining sculpture & manuscripts, the latter interesting me exceedingly.

Friday

Still the dense fog rested on the city but ventured out and in the afternoon landed at the Zoological Gardens when I saw nearly the entire collection of birds, beasts & reptiles.

Grace's Diary

Saturday

Thought to see the Houses of Parliament, but they were closed because of the fog. Being disappointed there I struck off for the Tower which I saw partially and finished the remaining portion open to visitors today (Monday).

Sunday

Heard Messrs Fullerton & Smith at the Metropolitan Tabernacle at the evening service. It was a novel sight to me to see that great temple packed to its roof with people.

Monday

Have been with Mary to see Mrs Rhodes at Forest Gate. Going we passed the Monument and (at my proposition) mounted to the top — 311 steps. What a grand view of London there must be from thence on a clear day. It has been a lovely day — though hazy. Am going tomorrow to Mrs Rhodes to spend the day.

Tuesday

Spent a very pleasant day at Rhodes'.

Wednesday

Called to inquire after the health of Miss Nightingale. She was visiting Sir Harry Verney, but was informed she is in good health. Coming over to Hyde Park walked along the banks of the Serpentine watching the skaters of whom there were thousands — saw the Albert Memorial — greatly pleased and interested by it.

Thursday, 8th Jan

Returned home from S. Pancras 12 p.m. Found all well and glad to welcome me home after my very pleasant & instructive holiday. School on Monday.

On the Census for 1891 Grace is listed as "Board School Certificated Teacher" living with her parents and Beaty in Albert Terrace, Market Street Lane, Belper (now Green Lane). John and Clara Dexter with children Hilda (5), Giovanni Hermon (1) and Clara's mother Annie Redmill are living on New Road. They were all involved with Belper Baptist Church, and John Snr. was an active member of the Building Committee for the new chapel.

Jany 23rd

Am writing in bed where I have been confined three days with a severe cold in my chest. Hope to get up tomorrow. Last Saturday sat for an examination (at Derby) in "Contemporary History", a scholarship having been offered by Mr W. J. Stead in 'The Review of Reviews' to the Competitor who scores best in the undertaking. I was the only one who presented myself for examination at the Derby "centre", but how many more sat in different places of the country — nay — the World, I cannot estimate. I wish I had worked more diligently in preparation for it. Not that I think to have stood a chance of winning the £300, but there are to be given in addition certificates of merit of which I might have possessed one but I fear my "paper" would not sufficiently merit such an acknowledgement. The result will be known in March.

I am back at Cow Hill working away in the usual routine of school life. I often think of London and wonder when and under what circumstances I may ever go there again. What histories might be written of the life & lives in such a place! I have been reading "The Old Curiosity Shop" for the first time. How interesting to me it has been, the more so from having just returned from the great scene of many such stories, if only they were written. Poor Little Nell! How I wept on coming to her death after so devoted and patient a life. It is a very beautiful life and character to contemplate, hers, so sweet, childlike, and yet strong, and full of purpose. It is easier to describe than to be such an one. I always enjoy Dickens — his humour, mirth here and there, touches of pathos suit me very well. It is a very hard winter, much frost, ice, and snow. I have skated three times.

Ap 24

Have had a glorious Mission Week. Rev. Thos. Cook at the Weslyan Chapel — stood up tonight with other Christians consecrating our lives afresh to the service of Christ — went with my dear sister-in-law into the inquiry room where she received forgiveness.

May 29

Have been in charge of school all week. Head mistress away ill — have had very little trouble anyway — am glad of the experience for future need. Visited two poor bedridden sisters, in adversity, this week with Mr Ling & Mrs Beresford — sang to them "Behold Me Standing at the Door"

(Sankey)[43] with which they professed themselves pleased. God has helped me in everything this week, and I go forth courageously in His strength.

June 17th

Miss Pine[44] returned this week after three weeks' absence. We have had staying with us Mr Russell from Mr C. H. Spurgeon's College, London. It has been a time of rich blessing to us both as a family, and as members of the Church. All our Baptist brethren are hoping he may return to be our pastor & evangelist. He is quite willing to come amongst us if Mr Spurgeon approves, and I do hope he will, feeling that he is just the man we want to stir us up, and by his example and earnest preaching to show us the reality of Christian life and teaching. I believe him to be a thoroughly sincere man, considering his every action as in the sight of God. It is indeed a privilege & blessing to have such a servant of God under our roof. The sweet fellowship we have had on eternal themes, family prayer, singing etc. has caused us to feel it has been good for him to be here. He has been with us ten days — returned last night to London — took a basket of flowers with him which my school children brought me. "How lovely are the messengers that preach us the Gospel of Peace." My brother John has applied for membership of the church, and I pray & trust he may be a very earnest supporter of the cause of Our Lord.

June 20

I sent Mr Russell a box of flowers, give me for him by Miss Walker (one of our teachers). They came just after he had gone, so I forwarded them & have received the following reply.

34 St George Street
Peckham, S. E.
19 June 1891

Dear Friend,
    Sincerely hope I have not brought myself into disgrace with Miss Grace through not writing before to say the box of lovely flowers arrived quite safely. Many many thanks to your kind friend for the gift and to yourself

---

[43]   "Behold me standing at the door " by Fanny Crosby, in Sankey's *Sacred Songs & Solos*.
[44]   Miss Harriet Frances Pine was Mistress at Cow Hill Board School, Belper (Kelly's TD 1891).

for sending them. I have a glass dish full, nicely arranged, with me in my study as I write. We are delighted with them as we were also with those brought home by me.

We had a grand day at the "Stockwell Orphanage" yesterday, but a gloom was cast over the proceedings by Mr Spurgeon's deeply regretted absence. I am sure we shall all pray that the Lord may see fit in His great mercy and goodness to restore him speedily.

Will you please give my warm Christian regards to your dear Mother & Mr & Mrs John Dexter not forgetting Beatrice also, and hoping Hilda & Herman are nicely & indeed that you are all quite well & hoping soon to send some definite news.

believe me, with sincere regards,

    Ever yours in Christ

      John Russell

N.B. Mr Russell didn't come to B[elper], Mr Spurgeon's illness preventing him. He is now in S. Africa.

Blackpool July 8

Have been here 3 days, return tomorrow. Came by the P. S. A. trip, spent the first day with our Sunday Evening Mission friends, Mr Smedley, Mrs Beresford etc. & am staying with Mr Bates & family of Belper in very nice apartments near the sea. I already feel like a different being. My face is <u>so</u> red. The sea here is grand — comes right on to the parade at high tide, it is delightful to watch. The waves come leaping over the breakwater & beach. Went yesterday a sail to Southport, which place I think very pretty as a town but prefer B. as a seaport on account of the <u>nearness</u> of the sea. The sands at S. extend so far, ′ ′ong walk to get to the water at all. But the sail was grand. Lovely ⁓ at all rough, though not quite calm. Got into conversatio⁓ ⁓ who travels thousands of miles on a journey, enjoyed t¹ , topics being democracy, division of land & politics ⁓ ⁓reshing to meet with a well-informed, communicati⁓ ⁓.m. off to Llandudno — now for a run on the sands ⊦ Saturd⁓ ⁓day at L., sun shining all day — reached the top of G⊦ ⁓w S. Ludo's Ch. and the grave of John Bright's[45] son on ⁓scription "And there shall be one fold & one shepherd."

Correction: page 65, last line but one: should read St. Tudno's, not St Ludo's.

Stood before the house in Lloyd St. where we stayed ten years ago with dear
Maria. Ah how quickly the time has gone. Had a splendid sail back — 4½
hrs, rough rather, but I was not sick either way. Came down the Gt. Orme
with one who had been in India, Italy, Switzerland etc. so had another
interesting chat. Today return to Lea with Mr Miers and daughters who are
bringing Mrs & Miss M__ a trip, so expect to have another happy day with
them.

Stayed at Chapel House, Lea till Wednesday evening having a very happy,
restful time — quite a delightful ending to my outing. The Miers family are
so refined in every respect. I enjoy so much visiting them. Met at their
home Mr Sewell & Miss Burt with whose society I was much pleased. Mr
S. being a good player on the piano. I sang one or two of "Messiah", as did
Miss B. Read life of George Eliott and part of Mr Ruskin's life.

Sep 15

I have been reading over what I have written on preceding birthdays since
my twentieth, and I believe I have been in a more enviable frame of mind on
all than at the present — I am passing through a very strange mental
experience just now — whether through my own fault or the conditions and
circumstances over which I have no control, I cannot say, but I know that
everything seems unsettled, nothing fixed upon which I can fully rely. I still
go on with my daily work of teaching, trying to fulfil my duties as well as I
can. I go to the P. S. E. Mission — sing occasionally, read the lesson but
do no visiting now nor often speak to the people. I am trying to solve
certain questions which, till I have come to a firm conclusion about, hinder
me from throwing myself into the work which I have always thought to be
right — that of helping those who are poor & suffering. But one must have
something absolutely definite before beginning the work, so it seems to me.
I may be wrong though. I feel as if I don't know anything. O, that I had
some one to talk to, to enlighten me if possible. I could not unburden my
heart to anyone here. I feel as if I would like to go away, among new
surroundings. Though the people we know here are very nice & many of
them very good, I feel they are not — at least I would like someone who
could understand me. I want to learn more, yet that does not give quiet to
one's mind. I think sometimes why can't I always be thinking. Have often

45   John Bright (1811-1889), Quaker reformer.

delightful solitary walks along the road to Ambergate. One spot there is where my soul rises in adoration to the Creator of its glories, more than any other place — the sun setting — his glowing rays reflecting in the clear, wide, silent river, trees in full green leaf dipping and swaying on either side — hills beyond clothed in summer luxuriance — many a time has my heart burst forth & been glad in contemplating this lovely scene — but then — the chills of doubt, uncertainty, reason unsatisfied. What is my poor reason after all — I wish I didn't allow it to assert itself so. Some people have such faith, never question anything. They must be far happier than the cold questioning people, as I.

Christmas 1891

Spending my holidays in Leicester. My cousins are so kind to me — cheerfulness & pleasure surround me — we are very poor at home just now but here is plenty and happiness. I have been here a week and am staying another — went to an evening party on Boxing Day and enjoyed myself very much — have invitations to others before returning home. I am now Secretary to the Belper Branch of the British Women's Temperance Association. We had a splendid meeting of women at Belper a fortnight ago, over ninety women sat down to tea — the President, Mrs J. Beresford, Miss Hunt and myself gave short addresses (my first) — we took several pledges. I do hope our branch will prove successful in the work.

New Year's Eve 12 o' clock

The bells are once more ringing out the old and in the new. I am in my bedroom retiring for the night — received today two nice letters from home — from my Mother & Sister. I have not written much here since last New Year's Eve. I wondered then what this year would bring forth — it has not been very eventful to me so far as I can see and again I look forward to /92 with expectation. I have gained my parchment certificate this year for which I am thankful.

❦1892❦

Feb 27 /92

Have been at home a fortnight laid up with influenza but am thankful to be able now to sit up in my bedroom to read, write etc. Such a many high & low in estate have been carried off by this epidemic — including HRH the Duke of Clarence — the death of so young a man and on the eve — as it were — of his marriage, causing the nation great sorrow and the profoundest sympathy with his relatives. Many whom we know personally and by repute have died all in so short a time, that one feels grateful for spared life amid such general cutting down. I have read several books while in bed including "The House & Its Builder" (S. Cox DD.), "The Programme of Christianity" (H. Drummond), "Wise Words & Loving Deeds" (G. Conder Gray) being a collection of short biographies of noble women, and "The History of the French Revolution" by Carlyle — which latter I have not read word by word, as everything seems so chaotic and bewildering. Yet I like his forcible style — so straight to the mark and powerful in description — but who can read of the Reign of Terror without feeling bound to close the book saying, "enough of such horrors." I like "Heroes & Hero Worship", have read it once and am going through it again. Have read some French too. I hope to be able to return to my school duties next week, shall ask the doctor today when I may go out, but one has to be very careful in this complaint, not to be too venturesome.

Mother had a very kind letter from Cousin Lizzie (Leicester) enquiring about me, and asking that I should go there when able "for a change", but I must relieve them at school as soon as possible for I know they have had a strain on them through my absence. I have so much to do when better, with temperance work, my own studies etc. The B. W. T. A. Secy (London) is continually sending notices which demand my attention. I do hope my health will sustain the pressure.

May 23rd 1892 Oversetts, Newhall, Nr Burton-on-Trent

This is where I am at present located, having been appointed Certif. Assistant Mistress at the Oversetts Board School[46]. It is quite a new

---

[46]   The Minutes of the Stanton & Newhall School Board (*Burton Chronicle*, April 14 1892) note that" Miss Dexter of Belper" had been appointed to Oversetts School. Known as the "Iron School", it was situated on Main St. Newhall, opposite the end of Oversetts Rd.

experience for me in many things. I have two rooms and board myself. I feel a bit lonely sometimes, but prefer being this to sharing rooms with another, for now I can be quiet and do as I wish. Then the school is large and mixed (boys & girls). I have to teach some things I have never been required to teach before as geography, history etc. but there, I shall get accustomed to in time. The work is greater than in the Belper schools — but I am having a larger salary so I must be prepared for increased duties. I have been here three weeks, and have been three Sundays to the Baptist Chapel at Swadlincote — about a mile & a half from here. Yesterday (Sunday) I enjoyed the services better than previous ones. Mr Bond, the pastor, I knew as a student. He seems thoroughly in earnest in his preaching and work and I feel that I shall get good under him. The friends at Chapel welcomed me very kindly, Mr & Mrs Cooper asking myself & Miss Gunson (one of the Assistants here whose home is in Scotland) to spend the afternoon with them which we did, feeling grateful for the notice they had taken of us as strangers.

On Thursday we go to Mrs Bond's. Miss G. was so delighted with our service that I think she will go regularly — she is a nice girl, and so far from home. At the end of next week I go home for Whitsuntide. I do so long to see my dear Mother's face. It seems we have been parted so long — what a baby I am yet and twenty-six! This is a colliery district, the people are tough, but, I believe, kindly and open. I trust it will prove of good, my coming here. I like the school master & teachers very well so far.

May 31st
Went to Mr Bond's on Thursday & had a very pleasant time — on Friday attended his art class at the Baptist Schoolroom — for design & painting. Two of our Assistant Mistresses, Miss Thrumpton & Miss Gunson, went with me. We drew a spray of ivy leaves from the board and were much amused by our first attempt. We are to do them from nature next time. Had a pleasant Sunday tea at Whitfields, chapel twice. Received another letter from my dear Mother today, which has given me much pleasure.

June 13th
Just returned from my week's holiday at home. We have had glorious weather. Monday, walked with Father, Mother & Mary to Whatstandwell through the woods & had tea at my brother's. Sunday went to Via Gellia

with Father, John & Clara, gathered bunches of lilies on the hillsides. It is a lovely spot. Wednesday visited the Miers family at Lea. Thursday, had a little party of friends to tea & supper. Friday, spent a quiet day with my Mother. Saturday went with Miss Annie Walker through the Belper Workhouse. The sights I saw in some cases made a sad impression on my mind, nevertheless, we were much interested in the organisation & general working of the place. Both Sundays were spent at home. Altogether I have had a very happy time.

June 19th, Skegness

My Mother and I are spending a little time together here. The place is very quiet for the weather has not been very warm and therefore there is a lack of visitors. I do wish the sun would come out. We went on Sunday to the Weslyan Chapel, and heard a grand preacher — Rev W. Jackson of London. He also gave a lecture last night on William Burley Puncheon to which we went. It was very humorous & also instructive. It is very restful & delightful to me to be here alone with my dear Mother. She was not at all well so proposed that we should come out together and she consented and seems already much better. We can see the sea well, from our windows. I have been out each morning before breakfast walking on the sands. O, this glorious sea, how it invigorates, expands, and strengthens one in every way. I do love it.

Aug 18th

Have been back at Newhall School nearly a fortnight. Mother & I stayed a week at Leicester after being at Skegness, so that all together we had a very pleasant outing. Aunt Jane went with us to Belper and stayed a short time. We were so glad to have her with us, such a dear, good kind Aunt as she is, and it is so long since she visited us. I shall not be here very long having already sent in my resignation to the Board. The class I have charge of is so backward and the children seem so hard to rouse to their work, the Master caning them frequently and strongly for ill performed tasks that I long to be away. I feel it may have been a mistake, my coming here, and yet it has perhaps been a necessary experience for me — certainly the needlework requirements have helped me to a practical demonstration of hitherto uncalled for qualifications, at least on so large a scale. I shall about have all finished (as to garments) by the end of the month. All is unknown yet as to where my next location will be. I prayed tonight earnestly to have my way divinely directed. Miss Gunson, one of the Assistants, is sharing my rooms. She is a nice fresh-coloured dark-eyed Scotch lassie and I am glad of her company.

Augst 27th

Just returned from Leeds, where I have been, at the request of the School Board, to attend a committee, as to an appointment. I can go there if I like, meantime I have one in London to attend next week. Am to let the L. Bd. know my decision by Thursday. I went through the Town Hall, a very fine building, the hall keeper being very kind & considering it quite a novelty for a lady alone to ask to be shown through the building. The Mayor's rooms are fine, so is the hall where the Musical festival will be held shortly. Next week there is a rehearsal. I would like very much to be there then. It has been a long day, nearly 200 miles train — very tired. Must go to bed. There are some good & fine pictures in the Art Gallery. One pleased me very much, "Milton dictating his Paradise Lost to his daughters", so pathetic!

Octr. 10th

When last I wrote, I said that I had a notice to attend a manager's meeting in London. Well I attended it, and was appointed as Assistant under the West Ham Board. I have always wanted to live in L. & when the opportunity offered I took it, and am now living at Stratford.

On leaving Newhall, I went home for a fortnight, during which time my brother's little baby Walter Raymond died. He was 13 months old. A dear, good-tempered, patient darling. I sat up with him two nights & felt that love which one only feels when nursing a tender little one. It was a blow. We seemed to do all in our power and then — all was unavailing. It is hard, but these mysterious providences, we must count our blessings, although it seems an impossibility to do so at the time. This is the third child my brother has lost. What trouble he has had to be sure. I only had one week at Belper, after this & for two days was in bed with bad throat etc. quite knocked up with over strain. On the Sat, I came up to Forest Gate to my friends Rhodes whom I have mentioned before. Monday morning started at the Abbey Schools, West Ham. They are the second largest in the United Kingdom. So this is a sort of distinction at last! Well, the Mistress is very nice, so are the teachers as far as I know. I teach the VI & VII Stds, the highest in the school. So this is another change. I have lived three weeks at Mrs Rhodes & now am in what I think will prove very comfortable lodgings at Mrs Garstang's, 55 Grove Crescent Rd. Stratford E.

The teachers have been very good in looking out for me in this respect, it is through one of them that I have come here. Now I have to attend a Science Class for Physiology & Hygiene so must be off. Last week, at Forest Gate Weslyan Chapel I heard Rev Hugh P. Hughes speak on "The London Mission" & last night at the same place a sermon by Mark Guy Pearse. Very powerful both were.

Oct 19

Last Saturday visited the Tel El Armana exhibition of M. Petrie (Oxford Mansion, Oxford St.) consisting of excavations from Egypt of remains of Akhenaton's Palace built B. C. about 1300. Many of the exhibits were in a perfect state of preservation, and showed the skill possessed by men, at that time of day, in carving, drawing, enamelling, moulding etc. Was deeply interested & instructed by going. Sent home a catalogue.

On leaving here, I struck across to the Abbey, where the newly-made tomb of Lord Tennyson, with the wreaths, one of laurels (entirely) by Queen Victoria was being visited by great numbers of people. We passed in single file by the grave while perfume from hundreds of flowers filled the edifice. So one more has gained his rest. Also crossed over to the Houses of Parliament. Went through all the various rooms, except the House of Lords which was being cleaned. Very splendid were the carving, gilding & painting, frescoes etc. The H of C was the most interesting to me. I know now which is the Front Opposition bench, Lobby etc. of which I have so often read & wished to see. If I could only hear a debate, but that even may come in time. I took my Elementary Singing Certif. on Friday. Last Sunday walked to the E. London Tabernacle — service good, preacher simple but pointed & powerful. I think I shall go there often, though it is a long way to walk to Mile End. Next Sunday I expect to hear the pastor, Rev A. Brown.

❧1893❧

Jany 6th 1893, Belper

The term of my Xmas Holidays is nearly expired. We have had a happy
time especially on Christmas Day. John, Clara & their two children came.
We had a splendid dinner, and all was joyous. A severe frost had continued
during the whole fortnight & we have had plenty of skating, on the fishpond
& the canal. Tomorrow I return to L[ondon]. It will be hard to part even
for a short time from my dear Mother, who gets to look much older. I can
see it more plainly with being away a time, but we may not be parted long. I
trust not, for she so looks to me for affection & comfort. God grant I may
be all in all to her in these her declining years. I sang at Crich on Boxing
Day the "Children's Home".[47] John gave a pianoforte solo & they were
much pleased with both performances. This lovely countryside has charmed
me more than ever in its winter glory. "All Thy works praise Thee, O God,"
all things, trees, hills, rivers, birds seem to say.

Jany 7th

Am back at Stratford again — left my darling Mother much upset by my
coming — have just written, hopefully, to her, bidding her cheer up & live
for my sake, praying that God may prosper & bless me that I may be able in
a small degree to recompense or rather to show my gratitude for all her great
love shown to me in every way. O, how I love & wish to cherish her — she
is the dearest, best of mothers that ever lived & loves me <u>so</u> much.

Feb 16th

Was received as a member of the East London Tabernacle & had the right
hand of fellowship from the Rev. Archibald G. Brown last Sunday evening.
I trust I may be of some good here. Today received a nice letter from Miss
Hume, late head mistress of Sneinton Board School, where I was
apprenticed as a P. S. She has been in London ever since she left there. It is
ten years since I saw her. Oh how delightful it will be to talk over old times.
I go to see her shortly. Our exam is over, the school did very well. Now I
am teaching St. I.

---

47   A popular song with a pathetic theme by F. H. Cowen.

Feb 26th

Sunday — Very wet — have been to a little mission room just across the way. Mr Neilsson is a most eloquent preacher. I went last Sunday & little expected in so humble a place of worship, when a discourse worthy of being delivered in the finest edifice in the land. His diction, reasoning & forceful way of putting the truths of the Gospel are excellent. I helped them in the Sunday School last week & am going again this afternoon. During this week I went to a meeting to hear Miss Kate Marsden lecture (with views) on Siberia & the lepers there, whom she has spent many a long month to find and help. Her devotedness is remarkable, considering the dangers, sufferings & discomforts of all kinds through which she has to pass in order to reach these poor outcasts from the abodes of men — but not from Christ, thanks be to Him — He healed them, when on earth, and is now inspiring these grand self-sacrificing women to "go & do likewise". She said nought but His presence & support could have kept her through all the trials of the way.

Thursday March 2nd

Sang "The Children's Home" at the mission room. We had a very good time there.

Saturday March 4th

Visited Miss Hume — had a delightful chat, reminiscences of schooldays etc. Heard her read a paper on "Charles Kingsley" at Dr Clifford's Chapel, which was most interesting & beautifully worded & put together. It was like a fresh country breeze refreshing to mind & spirit, this long wished for interview with my dear Mistress. She is just the same quiet loving intelligent woman. What a privilege to come into contact with such!

Sunday Mar 5th

This morning went all the way to Praed St to hear Mr Griffiths — Miss Hume told me he had been appointed Minister there, so I, longing to hear my old Minister again, went. About fifty in congregation. It seemed rather dull & deserted looking & I fancied, I felt sure, rather, that he had a desponding ring in his voice. Can it be that he is in difficulty, this was the test. "As thy day, so shall thy strength be," he said, we must pray before the evil day of sore temptation or temporal upsetting of any kind arrives, for in the very hour of darkness, we are or may be unable to offer up a prayer at all, then

Christ, whom we have previously entreated, comes to the help of his sore-tried one & rescues him. It appears a poor church or cause at P. St., but it is to be sincerely hoped he does not suffer because of this. Many strange necessitudes have been his. May God, in whom he so loyally & faithfully trusts cause brightness, joy & every temporal & spiritual blessing to a shower in rich abundance upon him — for he is a truly good man, I believe. Have just returned from the Sunday School. It has been good to be there too. One gains a further insight into Scriptural truths by teaching them to the dear children.

June 3rd

I so forget to write in here. Went home at Easter and also last week, Whitsuntide. They are in very low water there. My dear brother is having a hard uphill time with his new business, Father is helping him so there is very little cash coming in to Ivy Cottage. My poor Mother is much worried and distressed because of it. May things soon turn. I am getting on very well at "The Abbey". Miss Ware is delighted with my class. It is good to be appreciated when you try hard. Have sat for Physiology & Hygiene — hope to pass. When at home last week, went with Father, Mother, John, Clara, Beatie & the babes, Hermie & Hilda, in the "punt" along the canal, to have a tea-picnic in Lea Hurst Park. It was delightful — boiling the kettle with collected sticks, spreading the cloth, setting out the nice things we brought for tea — rowing or steering & acting as horse in the "punt" — climbing rocks amid ferns, wild flowers & trees — children's prattle — all so refreshing!

Then on Wednesday drove with Mr Mitchell to Wingfield Manor — had tea at the "Peacock". Young Mr Mounteray being a very good tenor, we had some music. One of the days to look back on as a rift in the clouds — "when the heavens are blue & the earth bright." On the top of a tower in the old ruins, my spirit so thankful, blessed God for the sweet, congenial seasons we are given to enjoy. Today have been to the Albert Hall to hear Adeline Patti. She is just about to retire. I was somewhat disappointed, though, in the Gallery, it is disadvantageous to hear. The Meister Glee Singers were a treat. Hyde Park was very good today, the keeping of the Queen's birthday. It is a strange world. I like London though it wearies one to see so many people & things at a time. Goodnight. Am sending my brother John a rose — his birthday — nothing else to send!

75

June 20th

On Sunday evening went to Praed St to hear Mr Griffiths. The same dear voice — earnest, true, faithful, sincere; old memories, feelings were stirred. O these hearts of ours why will they not rest but turn so to the past — sweet, yet bitter past. Would we have it return? Ah, no, not with the bitter, but the sweet — yes; but it cannot, we are changed, hurried along by circumstances, hardened, yet the tender spots are there, undiscovered, till the spring is touched. This is weakness to look back — "forward be our watchword," to new hopes, feelings, aspirations. Let the past be forgotten, the future be contemplated. He was glad to see me & asked after all at home — why was I here? because I liked London — life, activity, restlessness are here. I am so ambitious & love change. Why do I? Ah those contented quiet souls are much happier, my spirit yearns ever for the society of the refined & learned, yet on my path must be through drudgery & amongst the illiterate, but I am ignorant — so very — myself — what figure should I make in company erudite? Foolish thought — yet it will keep — and taking away my content. A poor woman whom I had the pleasure of visiting last night — though so poor in circumstances & in a consumption — was full of sweet contentment, full of the spirit of her Master, happy & thankful in such a condition. How such a spirit triumphs over its surroundings & is in the highest sense, noble and Godlike, but I am so human, weak worldly, material & cannot reach this atmosphere. My sister Clara has a new-born son — his name is to be Richard after my grandfather Dawkins, a good, kind man. I had sweet letters from two of my old school colleagues yesterday, Meddy Winterbottom & Mary Gunson. In my poor little bedroom I write yet, yet, ambitious heart, thou wouldst inhabit palaces. Such is a soul, illimitable in its reachings, deep in its longings, unsatisfied with less than infinitude.

Have just written to my dear Mother — why am I away from her — so loving a heart yearning for me — yet I go from it to strangers, buildings, the world. This does not satisfy — O, my God, show me the goal of my yearning soul.

June 25 1893 Sunday (afternoon)

Just returned from Conference Hall, West Ham Lane, where Mr Henry Varley has given an impressive address from S. Luke XIX 11-27. He is one now looking for the Second Coming & believes in the final punishment of

His (Christ's) enemies at that time. This is opposed to the doctrine or views held by the mission room friends, though I know very little of what they really believe only this — that "God is love & nothing else." Mr Varley spoke several times of the Wrath of God. He said all governments, whether absolute or limited monarchies or republics were & had been failures & would continue to prove so till the rule of the King of Righteousness. One hears strangely conflicting opinions expressed & the holders of them are, or appear to be, so confident of their rightness that it is impossible to get at absolute truth from man — for it seems that each is equally sincere in his beliefs. On Friday night went up West to S. James' Hall for the purpose of hearing a discussion between Mrs Besant & some other lady on Theosophy & Buddhism — found it is to be next Friday. Crossing to Prince's Hall was rewarded by hearing Lady Henry Somerset who, in a speech of delightful & flowing eloquence set forth & pleaded yet again the cause of Temperance. What a sweet, womanly, winning manner & smile she has, & it is so great a power in this work. Yesterday saw the Geological Museum, Jermyn St, quite alone though. This loneliness sometimes oppresses me & I long, oh so much for a kindred spirit, not for any other. Mr Neilsson is getting better & I am so thankful.

July 5th

Miss Ware left on Friday amid heartfelt regrets on the part of teachers & scholars. She gave each of us teachers a gold brooch, mine is in the shape of a fly — has five pearls & a ruby & is very pretty. We presented her with a handsome Davenport. She has been promoted to the Inspectorate of Schools so we shall occasionally see her. Miss Clive is our new Mistress. I had a sweet cheering letter from my beloved Mother this morning, telling me of her going with Father to the Baptist Conference at Derby & seeing Mr Griffiths who told them how well I looked & how glad he was to see me at his chapel. They saw Mr Matthews too — "the Minister" — as we call him & had a good time in hearing Dr Clifford & others. It rejoices me so when I hear of their having any such refreshment. Tomorrow is the wedding day of T. R. H. Prince George & Princess May. We have the day's holiday. Went to see Mr Neilsson & took some flowers.

Grace's Diary

July 7th

Yesterday had a delightful rest in the morning & afternoon, drawing, reading, sleeping with lovely July breeze fanning my "fevered brow". In the evening went to see the illuminations which were fine — the designs of some being very pretty (for England). The crowd was enormous — all along from Mansion House to end of Piccadilly — a real wedding crowd singing, laughing, making humorous remarks & generally behaving admirably though there were "rough bits" at times. Have just written to my Mother, in reply to her sweet, cheering letter. Shall soon see her now — in three weeks!

July 11th

Another nice letter from Meddie W. Am expecting every day news of result of Science Exam — palpitation at every step of postman!!! — what will it be?

August 6th, Belper

Spending holidays at home — passed in Physiology — so glad. One week has gone — tomorrow Bank Holiday. The memorial stones of the new Baptist Chapel here are to be laid so we are expecting a grand day. Went up to Whatstandwell during last week — Meddie called while I was there, had a nice walk with her on the canal bank. The country is in full leaf & freshness. Lovely bits of scenery present themselves in our walks, re-vivifying the tired "London teacher" & causing thrills of rapture & ecstatic heart throbs.

Thursday 9th Aug

The ceremony on Tuesday went off splendidly, it being one of the hottest days of this brilliant summer. Seven stones were laid & about £90 collected leaving only £640 to be raised in order to clear the entire cost. This is very good. We had a "balmy" time on Mr Bakewell's lawn prior to the evening meeting at which some excellent addresses were given by Revs Mills, Harris & Haslam. I sang "Consider the Lilies" (Topliff) Yesterday (Wednesday) I drove with Mr & Mrs Mitchell & Miss Shaw to Willersley Castle, the seat of F. C. Arkwright Esq., there being held a bazaar in aid of Cromford School Funds. The grounds — wherein were marquees erected for the exhibition of the beautiful articles for sale — are, it would seem, unsurpassed for natural beauty. The Vale of Matlock lying in all its loveliness beneath with the winding river Derwent at the base of the cliff. The great beech trees are a sight in themselves. The fairy lamps, at dusk, added "enchantment" to the scene in which we revelled for hours wandering from point to point of these picturesque grounds to gain fresh aspects of the Switzerland-like beauties around and beneath us. We had a terrible thunderstorm last night which aroused us all.

Aug 14th

On Saturday went to Matlock Bath Flower Show with Meddie — met several acquaintances. Coldstream Guards played beautifully — glorious day.

Sunday, drove with Mr Mitchell to Whatstandwell where he preached afternoon & night. I sang twice. We had tea at John's & drove back to B. in the still cool evening. The weather is intensely hot. What a good thing it is holiday time, it would be unbearable in school just now.

Aug 24th

School began on 21st. Weather not so hot. The parting with my sweet Mother on Sunday night was a trial, but it must be so for the present. Beatie & I took our tea to Ambergate woods last Saturday & had a delightful time together, listening to the Band in the field below, where the Flower Show was being held, gathering blackberries & then sauntering home in the lovely twilight — glorious hills on either side. While above the azure blue with its diamonds & crescent drew from our hearts expressions of gratitude, admiration & worship. The dear girl's mind in its opening was sweet to me. God bless her & give her every grace & virtue.

Saturday Aug 27th

Took steamer up the Thames to Kew — visited gardens which are very beautiful. Felt like remaining always in such a paradise, but one's feelings can seldom be gratified in such ways as that so perforce returned by train to Waterloo Station. The blow on the river did me much good, bringing colour to my — I fear — faded cheeks & for the time revivifying me. It is so pretty up there (or down there) — the winding stream banked by luxuriant trees & the quaint looking houses. Some of them appear to be very old —present an interesting picture. I thought of our Pirate forefathers, penetrating the heart of the country by this same stream. How changed the land to then! One gets an idea of the vastness of this London by travelling as I did yesterday from the extreme E. to the extreme W. (or nearly so). It impressed me deeply.

Sep 3rd

Went again by steamer to Gravesend. Much interested in seeing river traffic — lovely day — grand time, though still alone.

Sep 15th

My twenty-eighth birthday. This finishes the first "volume" of my journal, begun nearly ten years ago. Will a second cover another such period of my life? I received letters with small love-gifts from home & the dear little ones at school brought cards for me. Miss Clive is so very kind, I do love her. Miss Gracie Brown sailed yesterday for China as a missionary. We had a delightful farewell meeting. The only satisfying thing, I firmly believe, is constant, unswerving fidelity to the Christ of God, all else is secondary — science, arts, music, literature, all peace of heart & love comes only from communion with the Author & Giver of <u>true</u> peace & to feel our life to be lived well, is to be gained only by <u>doing His will & carrying out His purposes concerning us.</u> This is the conclusion at which I have arrived after much thought upon, & some experience of, the varied ways in which men & women strive for rest & happiness — "None save Christ can satisfy."

Finis

Grace Jane Dexter
all herein written by her own hand, 15/9/93

❧Postscript❧

Grace's hard work finally paid off and her Diary ends on a confident note: she is happy in her new job at the Abbey Schools, West Ham, and enjoying living in London at last. Some time in 1894 her family — John and Rebecca, Mary and Beaty — moved to "Bank View", Duffield, a few miles from Belper, from where, in 1901, Grace was married in Duffield Baptist Church to Londoner Herbert Walter Dupree, a Stone Dealer of Huguenot descent. Even Aunt Jane Dawkins, now aged 86, was present to witness the happy event. The Duprees lived in London and then retired to "Bella Vista", South Stoke, Bath, where Herbert died in 1945 and Grace followed at the great age of 98, on 16th March 1963. They had no children.

John Dexter Snr. died 4th October 1904 in Duffield, and his wife Rebecca in Leicester on 1st November 1911; probably at the home of her son, as it was her daughter-in-law, Clara, who was present at the death. The couple are buried in the churchyard of Duffield Baptist Church and their slate memorial may be seen against the south wall. Interestingly, both dates of death are incorrect which seems to imply that it was put in place some time afterwards, when memories had faded.

Mary married a William Slater in Duffield Baptist Church in 1902. She died 25th June 1943, aged 91 and is buried in Nottingham.

Beaty married Harry Radford in Derby in 1910 and they had one daughter, Florence Grace. Widowed in 1939, Beaty remained close to her Aunt Grace, dying in Derby on 9th August 1950.

John Samuel Esperance is a bit of a mystery but it is known that he and Clara followed their son, Giovanni Hermon, to South Africa and probably died out there.

LEA HURST.

◆Index◆

83